RESEARCHING LANGUAGE

Research in so̶ ̶ ̶ ̶ ̶to be̶ ̶frequ̶ ̶ ̶ ̶ ̶ ̶ ̶ ̶ ̶ ̶unequal power relationships. This book d̶ ̶ ̶ ̶ ̶s the possibi̶ ̶ ̶ ̶ ̶s of developing the research
process so that it benefits the subjects as well as the researcher.

The authors distinguish between 'ethical', 'advocate' and 'empowering'
approaches to the relationship between researcher and researched,
linking these to different ideas about the nature of knowledge, action,
language and social relations. They then use a series of empirical case
studies to explore the possibilities for 'empowering research'.

All qualitative social research depends to some degree on researching
language. The book is the product of dialogue between researchers
from a range of disciplines (anthropology, cultural studies, sociology
and linguistics). It can be read by researchers, teachers and students
across the social sciences, and, through its combination of philosophical
discussion, methodological recommendation and case-study illustration,
it provides guidance that is practical without being simplistic.

THE POLITICS OF LANGUAGE
Series editors: Tony Crowley, University of Southampton
Talbot J. Taylor, College of William and Mary,
Williamsburg, Virginia

'In the lives of individuals and societies, language is a factor of greater importance than any other. For the study of language to remain solely the business of a handful of specialists would be a quite unacceptable state of affairs.'

Saussure

The Politics of Language Series covers the field of language and cultural theory and will publish radical and innovative texts in this area. In recent years the developments and advances in the study of language and cultural criticism have brought to the fore a new set of questions. The shift from purely formal, analytical approaches has created an interest in the role of language in the social, political and ideological realms and the series will seek to address these new problems with a clear and informed approach. The intention is to gain recognition for the central role of language in individual and public life.

RESEARCHING LANGUAGE

Issues of power and method

*Deborah Cameron, Elizabeth Frazer,
Penelope Harvey, M. B. H. Rampton,
Kay Richardson*

London and New York

First published 1992
by Routledge
11 New Fetter Lane, London EC4P 4EE

Simultaneously published in the USA and Canada
by Routledge
a division of Routledge, Chapman and Hall, Inc.
29 West 35th Street, New York, NY 10001

Set in 10/12 pt Baskerville by
J&L Composition Ltd, Filey, North Yorkshire
Printed and bound in Great Britain by
Clays Ltd, St Ives

British Library Cataloguing in Publication Data
Researching language: Issues of power and method. –
(Politics of language)
I. Cameron, Deborah   II. Series
300.72

Library of Congress Cataloging in Publication Data
Researching language: issues of power and method / Deborah Cameron ...
[et al.].
p. cm. — (Politics of language)
Includes bibliographical references and index.
1. Linguistics—Methodology.   2. Linguistic informants.
3. Sociolinguistics.   I. Cameron, Deborah.   II. Series.
P126.R47   1992
410′.1—dc20   91–30978

ISBN 0–415–05721–3
0–415–05722–1 pb

CONTENTS

THE AUTHORS

Deborah Cameron is Lecturer in Literary Linguistics at the University of Strathclyde, Glasgow.

Elizabeth Frazer is Fellow and Tutor in Politics at New College, Oxford.

Penelope Harvey is Lecturer in Social Anthropology at the University of Manchester.

M. B. H. Rampton is Lecturer in Linguistics at the University College of Ripon and York.

Kay Richardson is Lecturer in Communication Studies at the University of Liverpool.

ACKNOWLEDGEMENTS

Several people helped us in different ways while we were working on this book. We particularly want to thank the following people: Roger Andersen (who, sadly, did not live to see the finished work), Jill Bourne, John Corner, Norman Fairclough and Amelia Rampton.

We are also grateful to the Lancaster Language, Ideology and Power Group and the Glasgow Language and Politics Group, for some stimulating discussion at our 1988 joint meeting in Liverpool.

1

INTRODUCTION

Researching Language is a collectively written book. It is not just a set of essays connected by a common theme, but a text conceived, shaped, drafted and redrafted over a period of several years by five researchers from different disciplines (anthropology, cultural studies, sociology and sociolinguistics) working in collaboration. This is not to imply that we can speak or would want to speak with a single, authoritative voice. Indeed, it will be obvious in later chapters that we differ in important ways. Rather it means that this book has emerged from a process of discussion: it is a dialogue rather than a series of monologues. In this introductory chapter we want to establish the common assumptions, beliefs, questions and concerns that enabled us to start talking and structured our talk.

What first brought us together was an interest in the politics of language and the politics of researching it. We began to meet as a group soon after a conference in Lancaster in 1986 on linguistics and politics: an event that had highlighted issues of power which are often marginalised in sociolinguistics. The particular issue that interested us was to do with the politics of the research process itself. All of us had previously undertaken research in situations characterised by inequality, and we had therefore had occasion to ask whether research could be used to 'empower' actors in unequal situations.

Although the actual research projects presented in later chapters were already completed, or nearing completion, when we began to explore this question together, we decided we could use them as 'case studies', as material for our reflections. It follows – and this is a point we will emphasise repeatedly – that they are not intended as models or recipes for what we will refer to as 'empowering research'. They are the concrete basis and the experiential background to our exploration of what empowering research might be.

It is important to point out that the question we asked – whether and how research could be used to the benefit of both researcher and researched – is in some ways an obvious concern for any social scientist

1

to have, while at the same time it is a delicate matter and not at all straightforward. Some of the problems involved arise out of the history of the social sciences, and this requires more detailed comment.

POWER/KNOWLEDGE: THE POLITICS OF SOCIAL SCIENCE

As many commentators have pointed out – perhaps the fullest and most insistent statement can be found in the various works of Michel Foucault – social science is not and has never been a neutral enquiry into human behaviour and institutions. It is strongly implicated in the project of social control, whether by the state or by other agencies that ultimately serve the interests of a dominant group.

As a very obvious illustration, we may notice what an enormous proportion of all social research is conducted on populations of relatively powerless people. It is factory workers, criminals and juvenile delinquents as opposed to their bosses or victims who fill the pages of social science texts. Doubtless this is partly because members of powerful elites often refuse to submit to the probing of researchers – their time is valuable, their privacy jealously guarded. But it is also because a lot of social research is directly inspired by the need to understand and sometimes even to contain 'social problems' – the threats (such as crime or industrial disruption) that powerless groups are felt to pose to powerful ones.

Foucault observes, putting a new spin on the familiar saying 'knowledge is power', that the citizens of modern democracies are controlled less by naked violence or the economic power of the boss and the landlord than by the pronouncements of expert discourse, organised in what he calls 'regimes of truth' – sets of understandings which legitimate particular social attitudes and practices. Evidently, programmes of social scientific research on such subjects as 'criminality' or 'sexual deviance' or 'teenage motherhood' have contributed to 'regimes of truth'. In studying and presenting the 'facts' about these phenomena, they have both helped to construct particular people ('criminals', 'deviants', 'teenage mothers') as targets for social control and influenced the form the control itself will take.

We could consider, for example, the medico-legal discourses interpreting but also, crucially, regulating the behaviour of women. Recently, some acts of aggression by women have been explained as a consequence of hormonal disturbance ('pre-menstrual syndrome'); conversely, some instances of women drinking while pregnant have been explained (and indeed punished) as acts of conscious negligence (since they may lead to problems for the newborn, most seriously 'foetal alcohol syndrome'). There are two things to note here. One is that although the categories 'pre-menstrual syndrome' and 'foetal alcohol syndrome' are presented as objective and value-free scientific discoveries, it is clear that these new pieces of knowledge function as forms of social control over women. The other is that although they may seem to contradict one another (since one makes women less responsible for damage they cause while the other makes them more responsible than in the past) they nevertheless complement each other at a higher level of analysis: they fit and reinforce the logic of that broader control-discourse feminists call 'sexism'.

This interplay of power and knowledge (Foucaultians write 'power/ knowledge') and the historical link between social science and social control pose obvious dilemmas for the radical social scientist. We have to recognise that we are inevitably part of a tradition of knowledge, one which we may criticise, certainly, but which we cannot entirely escape. Even the most iconoclastic scholar is always in dialogue with those who went before. Our own disciplines, anthropology, sociology and linguistics, have problematic histories. Scholars of language and society may be less powerful than lawyers and doctors, but we have certainly contributed to 'regimes of truth' and regulatory practices which are hard to defend.

It cannot, for instance, be dismissed as coincidental or unimportant that three of the four case histories in this book involve white researchers working in non-white communities. It has been argued that historically, this structure whereby 'we' study 'them' has been institutionalised in the disciplines we represent, and that practitioners of those disciplines have been trained to perceive it as natural; they may have experienced some pressure to repeat it, in order to contribute to 'important' scholarly debates.

While this is a claim that must be borne in mind, we would have some reservations about the more extreme versions of it: as we will try to demonstrate later in this chapter, there is more going on in the relation between a researcher and those she researches than a simple racist or imperialistic 'us' versus 'them' opposition; and there may still be problems of power even when researcher and researched are not divided by cultural difference (as when Black researchers work in Black communities, for example).

It has also been argued that the content of the tradition is as problematic as its form. In some instances, the study of non-European languages and cultures, of creoles, and of working-class linguistic varieties, has formed a significant thread in western discourse about 'primitive' culture and racial inferiority, and in victim-blaming educational theories. In other instances the interventions of linguistic researchers have seriously disrupted cultural patterns among the researched.

3

The most notorious example of this disruption concerns the activities of the Summer Institute of Linguistics, a Christian organisation based in the USA which constructs grammars and writing systems for previously undescribed and unwritten languages. The SIL's avowed primary aim is to translate the Bible into indigenous vernaculars and make the people literate so they can read it. But as well as introducing a coloniser's religion, the SIL literacy campaigns serve colonialism in other ways: Peter Muehlhausler observes that the newly written language becomes a vehicle for colonial ideas rather than for recording indigenous ones. Worse still, 'in more than a few instances [in Polynesia, Micronesia and Melanesia] one of the first uses to which literacy was put was to sign away traditional lands to a coloniser' (Muehlhausler 1990: 190). He also points out that the long-term effect of vernacular literacy in the Pacific has been language death, since vernacular literacies tend to be transitional, and once people can read and write the circumstances are ripe for the coloniser's language to take over completely. The SIL could with justification be accused of destroying the linguistic ecology and local traditions of the regions in which it operates, very often in the interests of the US government and other agents of colonial capitalism.

In the light of examples like this, it would be quite irresponsible to deny the real effects of research in our disciplines or to play down the contribution they have made to maintaining and legitimating unequal social arrangements. And in this light, our hopes of 'empowering' the subjects of linguistic research might start to look at best naïve. Perhaps it would be better to stop doing social science research altogether?

The questions of how 'empowering' social research can hope to be, and whether in the end certain kinds of research should be undertaken at all are certainly serious ones, to which we will return directly and indirectly throughout this book: the answers, if there are any clear answers, cannot be pre-empted at this stage. For us, though, the starting point was that we had done research in situations of inequality, and we felt a need to reappraise critically the ways we had gone about it, making explicit issues of method that were not necessarily foregrounded at the time. In the following chapters, we ask questions in retrospect about why particular methods were used and to what extent they worked, or could have worked, towards empowering research subjects.

All of us were looking in our research at the ways in which particular disadvantaged groups used language, and we shared the conviction that this is, in one way or another, a politically significant area of study. Linguistic interaction is social interaction, and therefore the study of language use is fundamental to our understanding of how oppressive social relations are created and reproduced. If, as we believed, the politics of language is real politics, it is at least worth considering whether knowledge about it could be framed in a way that research subjects themselves would find relevant and useful.

THEORETICAL ISSUES: THE STATUS OF ACADEMIC KNOWLEDGE

Our early discussions of how research on language might empower its subjects raised general theoretical questions in two main areas: one was the status of academic knowledge itself and the other concerned the relation between researcher and researched in the making of know-ledge. We will begin with the first area, since, in it, important philo-sophical issues are at stake that relate very clearly to the questions to be raised when we come to the second area. Though they are not always discussed explicitly, these issues are fundamental to all empirical research, not just linguistic research. Epistemological assumptions deter-mine the way in which a researcher interacts with the researched: thus they influence methods and indeed research findings.

Quantitative sociolinguistics provides a clear example of epistemologi-cal assumptions affecting methods. Here we have a paradigm in which researchers want to gather data on language use from which its general rules can be induced. Accordingly, they are preoccupied with the 'observer's paradox', the idea that good quality data entail careful recording by an outside investigator, who none the less should ideally be absent from the scene in case she influences or interferes with the behaviour of the speakers being recorded. This implies that, ideally, researchers would produce wholly objective representations of reality. Of course sociolinguists recognise that they will always fall short of the ideal, but still they make efforts to distance themselves as far as possible from the researched and deliberately attempt to reduce or transcend interference.

Our own case studies demonstrate that researchers cannot help being socially located persons. We inevitably bring our biographies and our subjectivities to every stage of the research process, and this influences the questions we ask and the ways in which we try to find answers. Our view is that the subjectivity of the observer should not be seen as a regrettable disturbance but as one element in the human interactions that comprise our object of study. Similarly, research subjects themselves are active and reflexive beings who have insights into their situations and experiences. They cannot be observed as if they were asteroids, inanimate lumps of matter: they have to be interacted with.

The difference between our position and the position of someone who minimises contact with her subjects to avoid 'interference' is ultimately a difference in epistemology, the theory of what and how we can know. The two positions need to be placed in their theoretical context before

5

we proceed to relate them in detail to considerations of method. Therefore, we will go on to distinguish a number of approaches or 'isms', which differ in their conceptions of reality, the object of knowledge, and therefore in their opinions about how it can be described and explained. Initially we will distinguish two broad categories among scientists and social scientists: those who subscribe to *positivism* and those who do not. Among the non-positivists we will further distinguish between *relativist* and *realist* approaches.

It must be acknowledged that positivism, relativism and realism are complex positions whose definition is contested rather than fixed. Our presentation of them will simplify the picture by describing a sort of 'ideal-typical' position rather than the nuances of any specific theorist's actual position. The point of simplifying is to avoid getting bogged down in disputes about the 'real meaning' of our three labels or in the details of their histories in the philosophy of science. We are less concerned with terminology and much more concerned to draw some fundamental distinctions among theories of knowledge as clearly as we can.[1]

Positivism

Positivism entails a commitment to the study of the frequency, distribution and patterning of observable phenomena, and the description, in law-like general terms, of the relationships between those phenomena. To take a well-worn example, a postivist description of a game of billiards would refer to billiard balls rolling about at different velocities, colliding with each other and with the sides of the table, taking on new directions and speeds which are predictable and can be calculated using the laws of classical mechanics. The only real entities in this scenario are the balls, cues and table; but not the forces of friction, inertia and gravity (and there never seem to be any billiards players in positivist discussions of the scene). Positivism is strongly averse to postulating the reality of entities, forces or mechanisms that human observers cannot see. Such things are myths, mere theoretical inventions which enable us to predict and explain observable events but cannot be seen as the stuff of reality itself. At the same time, positivism is strongly committed to the obviousness and unproblematic status of what we *can* observe: observations procured in a scientific manner have the status of value-free facts.

This distinction between fact and value is important. Though confident that there are methods which can provide a clear view of reality, positivism is very much aware of the potential for observation to be value-laden, especially in the social as opposed to natural sciences. Indeed, for many it is a mark of 'pseudoscientific' theories like marxism and psychoanalysis that their adherents will see what they want, or what the theory dictates they should; such theories are shot through with political bias. Nor can you set up a controlled experiment to test Marx's hypothesis that the class in society which owns the means of production will also have control of political and cultural institutions by virtue of their economic dominance. It might well be true that there are no known counterexamples to Marx's statement, but we still cannot say that the statement itself holds up. It would be difficult to set out to falsify this statement, as positivism requires, because so many variables are involved and there seems to be no way of isolating and manipulating the relevant one. Because it does not provide us with hypotheses that can be in principle falsified, marxism for strict positivists is a pseudoscience rather than a science.

In sociolinguistics, the problem of the observer's paradox arises directly from the positivist emphasis on value-free observation as a possible and desirable goal.[2] Of course, the distinction between fact and value is of wider concern in the social sciences. Certainly, there are examples in physical science where observation – mediated often by the use of instruments like microscopes, stains and slides – does change what is observed. But when the object of observation is human behaviour the problem is endemic. Speakers who know a phonetician wants to measure their speech-sounds modify those sounds, even without being aware of it; consumers who respond to questionnaires never 'tell it like it really is', but alter their answers in deference to the interviewer or make themselves out to have social identities they do not have.

For these reasons, researchers try to devise methods that allow them to observe things 'as they really are'. Social interaction can be observed through a two-way mirror; tape recorders can be concealed or respondents can be asked their opinions about washing powder when the researcher is really sampling their vowel-sounds for future measurement. Social scientists may also disguise their purposes by pretending to be part of the group they are studying, a religious congregation, say. Circumventing the observer's paradox often involves the researcher in concealing herself and/or her purposes from those she is studying.

Challenges to positivism

Positivism is the 'hegemonic' position, the one scientists have generally been taught to regard not as a scientific method but as *the* scientific method. That is why we have grouped alternative positions as 'challenges to positivism': however different they may be from one another, they are obliged to define themselves first and foremost in opposition to positivism, the dominant 'common sense' of modern science. As this section makes clear, though, the two main challenges we identify – relativism and realism – are by no means 'the same thing'.

Relativism

Relativism does not recognise the observer's paradox as a problem because relativism does not recognise the fact/value distinction. Reality for a relativist is not a fixed entity independent of our perceptions of it. Our perceptions in turn depend on (are relative to) the concepts and theories we are working with whenever we observe. We invariably have some preconceived notion of what is there to be seen, and it affects what we actually see. Thus someone training as a doctor, say, has to learn to see in a different way: the 'reality' she sees in a chest X-ray is different from what she saw before she did her training, and different again from what a traditional healer from a non-allopathic perspective would see. The history of ideas and the sociology of knowledge provide many examples of scientific theories having close links with the moral and cultural values of their time and place.

Dale Spender (1980) cites a good example of how language plays a part in linking scientific theories with social assumptions. Psychologists investigating people's visual perception discovered two ways of responding to a figure on a ground: abstracting it from its context (the ground) or relating it to its context. These responses were labelled 'field independence' and 'field dependence' respectively. They were also associated with the behaviour of male subjects ('field independence') and female subjects ('field dependence'). Spender's point is that it is not a coincidence that the male-associated strategy was given a label implying a more positive evaluation – 'independence' is conceived as both a positive and a male characteristic. The female tendency could have been called 'context awareness' and the male tendency 'context unawareness'. That this alternative did not occur to the scientist has nothing to do with the nature of his findings about visual perception, and everything to do with his social preconceptions (i.e. he took it for granted that the positive term must be accorded to what men do).

Relativism in the social sciences particularly addresses the role of language in shaping an actor's social reality, as opposed to merely reflecting or expressing some pre-existent, non-linguistic order. The 'Sapir–Whorf hypothesis of linguistic relativity' has inspired a great deal of discussion on the language dependence of social reality. As Sapir argued:

> The fact of the matter is that the 'real world' is to a large extent unconsciously built up on the language habits of the group. No two languages are ever sufficiently similar to be considered as representing the same social reality. The worlds in which different societies live are different worlds, not the same world with different labels attached.
>
> (Sapir 1949: 162)

Subsequently, many social theorists and philosophers in the pheno-
menological tradition have stressed that social order exists *only* as a
product of human activity. For some, this can even mean that there is no
social reality, no facts, other than the actor's subjective experience.

Ethnomethodology is a development of this tradition which illustrates
both the strengths and the weaknesses of relativism. Ethnomethodology
takes very seriously indeed the actor's subjective experience of a situation, to the point of denying any other reality. In particular, it is hostile
to the marxist notion of historical forces determining actors' lives, and to
the structuralist postulation of social structures which coerce people into
social roles and hierarchical relations. In this view, a social researcher is
just like anyone else, an actor experiencing a situation: all research can
really ever amount to is the reporting of one's experience. Clearly, this is
an extreme anti-positivist position.

The problem here, though, is that in their zeal to emphasise the actor's
own role in constructing a social world, ethnomethodologists have left us
with a picture which implies that social actors could in principle
construct the world exactly as they pleased. More precisely, they have
given no account of why we cannot do this.

What makes this problematic? Very crudely, you might say it is a
variant of not being able to see the wood for the trees. Indeed, since they
deny the existence of higher-level social structures or social forces that
the individual actor is unaware of, ethnomethodologists must be sceptical of the idea that the trees in any sense add up to a wood. For them
there is no 'big picture' into which the study of some particular
phenomenon like a tree must be fitted.

We can put the point a bit more technically. Ethnomethodology is one
of those approaches that emphasise the 'micro' level of social organisation – a single interaction between two people, say – over the 'macro'
level of institutions and classes, and so forth. In contrast to positivists,
who conceive of explanation as stating general statistical regularities,
ethnomethodologists give explanatory weight to the subject's account of
herself. This means that if a woman says something like 'being a woman
has made no difference to my life', the ethnomethodologist has no
theoretical warrant for invoking the macro-category of gender. Here
the ethnomethodologist is reacting against the marxist idea of 'false
consciousness', which implies that people are entirely deluded about the
circumstances of their lives and that nothing a subject says should be
taken at face value. Ethnomethodologists find this too deterministic (as
well as condescending). For them, the way things are is the way subjects
say they are.

For us, though we do not necessarily embrace the idea of false
consciousness, this absolute faith in the subject's own account poses
very serious problems. We do want to pay attention to actors' own

understandings – a point we will follow up shortly – but do we want to give them the last word in every case? We would prefer to say that whatever they say, people are not completely free to do what they want to do, be what they want to be. For we would want to claim that on the contrary, social actors are schooled and corrected, they come under pressure to take up certain roles and occupations, they are born into relations of class, race, gender, generation, they occupy specific cultural positions, negotiate particular value systems, conceptual frameworks and social institutions, have more or less wealth and opportunity ... and so on, *ad infinitum*. As Berger and Luckmann say (1967), social reality may be a human product but it faces humans like a coercive force. It is a grave weakness of ethnomethodology, and more generally of relativism, that it offers no convincing account of that fact.

This critical view of relativism brings us closer to a 'realist' position, arguing that there is indeed a social reality for actors and researchers to study and understand.

Realism

Realism, like relativism, accepts the theory ladenness of observation, but not the theory-dependent nature of reality itself. Realism posits a reality existing outside and independent of the observer, but also stresses that this reality may be impossible to observe or to describe definitively.

Realism parts company with positivism on the question of reality being only what we can observe. Neither the social order nor gravity can be observed, and therefore in positivist terms neither is 'real' (strictly speaking, only the observable effects of a gravitational field are real; the gravitational field for positivists is an artificial theoretical construct). Realism, as its name suggests, is committed to the notion that things like gravity *are* real, though at any time an observer might describe them incorrectly and so give a misleading or mistaken account of their real character. It follows, too, that for realism explanation is more than just stating regularities or predicting outcomes (the positivist model). When a realist describes the workings of gravity she believes she is giving an account of how the world works and not just stating what would be likely to happen if you conducted a particular operation in the world.

In the philosophical project of deciding what counts as 'real' – atoms and molecules, tables and chairs, rainbows, societies, classes and genders – there is still everything to play for. The area is full of ambiguities: for example, does the Sapir–Whorf hypothesis imply that reality itself is linguistically determined, or that actors' experience of it, their 'mental reality', is? Commentators have expressed differing opinions on this. And does a 'mental reality' count as 'real'? These are hard questions, and philosophers have not resolved them.

What is hard to dispute, though, is the proposition that whatever the ultimate status of 'social reality', it is, partly at least, a *human* product. The continuing existence of such phenomena as social rules, behavioural rituals, institutions e.g. marriage and government, is dependent on human action. Human action maintains these phenomena, and they are therefore susceptible to change and transformation by human beings.

THE STUDY OF SOCIAL REALITY

The challenges to positivism we have just considered have implications for the study of social reality. For if the experience of social actors is language and culture dependent, and if we grant that there are many languages and cultures, a number of problems for social science present themselves at once.

To begin with, and whether or not she believes it has an independent objective reality, the social researcher cannot take it for granted that she knows or recognises exactly what a social phenomenon or event is when she sees it. A woman turning over the earth in a flower bed with a spade might immediately be understood by an observer to be 'digging the garden'. In fact, though, the digger's own understandings and intentions would be an important part of the reality – she might not be gardening, but preparing to bury the budgie. Even if she were gardening, the observer who simply recorded this might miss some very important aspects of the scene: the gardener might be letting off steam after a row with her children, relaxing after a hard day at the office or worshipping the Goddess Earth by cultivating her. These meanings are properly a part of the reality being observed; the question 'what is going on here' cannot be answered without reference to the agent's own understanding of what she is doing.

If there are problems discovering exactly what is going on in one's own backyard, so to speak, if the objective and non-interactive observation assumed by positivism as the ideal is impossible or useless even so close to home, the problems for social scientists who study cultures and social groups not their own are even more acute. There are two main problems: the existence of differing and shifting conceptual frameworks, and the difficulty of translating from one to another. Can the researcher situate herself within the conceptual framework of the researched and thereby understand what is going on? And can she give an account of this 'otherness' for an audience of readers who can relate to her (original) conceptual framework but not the framework of her subjects? We might be alive to the dangers of ethnocentrism, but in the end, can anything be done about it?

Some influential philosophers have replied in the negative, arguing that there are no universally valid standards by which to judge the rightness or wrongness of belief systems; conceptual frameworks cannot validly be compared. This is a strongly relativist position. It has also been strongly opposed by those who argue that there is in fact a fundamental level of shared human experience and concepts. We are all sentient, rational beings who inhabit a world of solid objects: we must all have an understanding of the continued existence of objects in time and space, of cause and effect, and so on.[3] Given such a 'bridgehead' between different human societies it is not so hard to see how we come to understand that someone else can have a different idea from ours of what causes rain, for instance. In other words, it is at least arguable that even radically unfamiliar conceptual frameworks can come to make sense to the observer.

But whether or not one holds an extreme relativist position, this debate highlights the problem that social reality is not just transparent to the observer. The social scientist must validate her understandings and interpretations with the community of researchers of which she is part (thus again raising the issue of theory-dependence in social scientific observation), but also and crucially she must validate her observations with the actors being observed. Asking what people are doing and why, as social scientists must, makes interaction with them inescapable.

You cannot validate a particular observation simply by repeating it. However many questionnaires you give out or interviews you conduct, it is impossible to be sure that all respondents who gave the 'same' answer meant the same thing by it, and that their responses are a direct representation of the truth. Furthermore, since persons are social *actors* the researcher cannot treat descriptions of their behaviour as chains of cause and effect, in the way one might describe the motion of billiard balls. To be sure, there are regularities to be discovered in the social world, but they are there because of people's habits, intentions, understandings and learning. Social scientists have to be concerned with what produces regularities as well as with the regularities themselves; and once again, this implies interaction with the researched.

This philosophical discussion on the nature of reality and the status of observation has been drawn out at length because it impinges very directly on the study of language use. It will be clear by now that we would argue that linguistic research is always social research. Though some currents in linguistics have treated language as a natural and self-contained phenomenon – even the recent 'modularity thesis' posits a self-contained ('autonomous') grammar interacting with other systems to produce the complexities of behaviour – the fact remains that language is only ever produced or interpreted in a social context. In the study of language use, therefore, positivistic 'objective' research methods are quite inappropriate. This means that the study of language use, in whatever academic discipline, cannot ignore actors' own concepts, descriptions and understandings of reality. Nor can the study of language use be detached from the social and political context in which language is used.

THE RELATIONS BETWEEN RESEARCHER AND RESEARCHED: ETHICS, ADVOCACY AND EMPOWERMENT

So far, we have focused on the general philosophical issues that arise in empirical research in social science, showing that social scientists may have very different goals – and consequently, use different methods – depending on what epistemological assumptions they make. As we have already pointed out in general terms several times, these differing goals and methods also entail different relations between researcher and researched.

In this section we will pay close attention to exactly that issue. We will distinguish three positions researchers may take up *vis-à-vis* their subjects: ethics, advocacy and empowerment. We will argue that ethics and advocacy are linked to positivist assumptions, while the more radical project of empowerment comes out of relativist and realist understandings. We will consider in some detail what is meant by 'power' and 'empowerment', ultimately introducing the kind of questions we must address in later chapters: questions about the empowering potential of methods like those we have used in our own work.

Ethics

The potentially exploitative and damaging effects of being researched on have long been recognised by social scientists. We touched earlier on one important source of potential damage, the way social science is used within regimes of truth, or directly for social control. Even when you do not work for a government agency, and whatever your own political views, it is always necessary to think long and hard about the uses to which findings might be put, or the effects they might have contrary to the interests of subjects. If a researcher observes, for example, that the average attainment of some group of schoolchildren is less than might be anticipated, that can colour the expectations of teachers and contribute to the repetition of underachievement by the same group in future. That might be very far from what the researcher intended, but an ethically aware social scientist will see the possible dangers and perhaps try to forestall them.

A second worry is that the researcher might exploit subjects during the research process. One controversy here concerns the acceptability of covert research, in which subjects cannot give full informed consent because the researcher is deliberately misleading them as to the nature and purpose of the research, or perhaps concealing the fact that research is going on at all. For instance, a great deal of research in social psychology relies on subjects thinking the experimenter is looking for one thing when she is really looking for something else. Some sociological studies have involved the researcher 'passing' as a community member; and some sociolinguists have used the technique of getting subjects to recount traumatic experiences because the surge of powerful emotions stops them from being self-conscious about their pronunciation, circumventing the observer's paradox. In cases like these one wonders how far the end justifies the means. Even when the deception is on the face of it innocuous, it raises ethical problems because it is a deception.

A famous example where researchers misled their subjects is provided by the Milgram experiments on obedience to authority: subjects were ordered to give other people severe elecric shocks, but in fact the people who appeared to suffer pain were the experimenter's accomplices, and the shock equipment was bogus. Comments on ethics with regard to this particular study tend to focus on the moral standards of the subjects, who revealed themselves in most cases willing to inflict severe pain because they were ordered to do so. It is less often asked how ethical the researcher was in lying to his subjects, subjecting them to severe stress and in all likelihood undermining their self-esteem when they discovered what the real point of the experiment was.

Most disciplines, government and other research agencies (including universities), do indeed have a strong concern with ethical standards, manifested by published codes of conduct, professional oaths, ethics committees, and so on. These work on the basis of balancing as fairly as possible the needs of a discipline in its pursuit of knowledge and truth with the interests of the people on whom research is conducted. The interests of the researched are a negative force limiting what researchers can do. Apart from preventing the abuse of subjects, an ethical researcher will be advised to ensure that their privacy is protected (e.g. by the use of pseudonyms when the findings are published) and where appropriate to compensate them for inconvenience or discomfort (whether in cash, as commonly happens in psychology, or in gifts, as from anthropologists to a community, or in services rendered, as with many sociolinguistic studies).

In ethical research, then, there is a wholly proper concern to minimise damage and offset inconvenience to the researched, and to acknowledge their contribution (even where they are unpaid, they will probably be thanked in the researcher's book or article). But the underlying model is one of 'research *on*' social subjects. Human subjects deserve special ethical consideration, but they no more set the researcher's agenda than the bottle of sulphuric acid sets the chemist's agenda. This position follows, of course, from the positivist emphasis on distance to avoid interference or bias. However, it is also open to positivistically inclined researchers to go beyond this idea of ethics and make themselves more directly accountable to the researched. They may move, in other words, to an *advocacy* position.

Advocacy

What we are calling the 'advocacy position' is characterised by a commitment on the part of the researcher not just to do research *on* subjects but research *on and for* subjects. Such a commitment formalises what is actually a rather common development in field situations, where a researcher is asked to use her skills or her authority as an 'expert' to defend subjects' interests, getting involved in their campaigns for healthcare or education, cultural autonomy or political and land rights, and speaking on their behalf.

A notable and relevant example of this kind of accountability in linguistic research is the case of the Ann Arbor 'Black English' trial in 1979. A group of African American parents in Ann Arbor, Michigan, brought a suit against the city schools for their failure to acknowledge and address the specific educational needs of children whose first language was American Vernacular Black English (AVBE). Children were being tracked into slow or learning disabled groups when their problem was in fact linguistic, a mismatch between standard English and the highly divergent AVBE which teachers had not understood.

It was crucial in pursuing the case that AVBE could be shown to be a recognisable, systematic and highly divergent (from Standard English) variety common to African American communities throughout the USA and resulting from the community's history of slavery and segregation. In order to show this, the community sought the help of sociolinguists who had studied AVBE and other Black Englishes. Linguists such as Geneva Smitherman played an important part in organising the campaign and recruiting other experts to it.

One of those who acted as an expert witness in the case was the (white) sociolinguist William Labov. In 1982 Labov published a retrospective account of the Ann Arbor affair, 'Objectivity and commitment in linguistic science', which has become a canonical statement on the social responsibility of linguistic researchers.

Labov suggests two principles. One is the principle of 'error correction': if we as researchers know that people hold erroneous views on something, AVBE for example, we have a responsibility to attempt to correct those views. (This, incidentally, is a clear example of 'commitment' and 'objectivity' serving the exact same ends; Labov believes in or is committed to putting truth in place of error.) The second principle is that of 'the debt incurred'. When a community has enabled linguists to gain important knowledge, the linguist incurs a debt which must be repaid by using the said knowledge on the community's behalf when they need it. This is clearly an advocacy position.

Labov further stresses that the advocate serves the community, and that political direction is the community's responsibility. As an outsider, Labov accepts – and counsels others to accept – an auxiliary role. 'They [linguists] don't claim for themselves the right to speak for the community or make the decision on what forms of language should be used' (Labov 1982: 27).

In the case studies that follow, both Ben Rampton (chapter 2) and Deborah Cameron (chapter 5) take up some of the problems Labov's statement raises. Here we will do no more than refer to a couple of them briefly. The important point we want to make is that while Labov's position is in some ways extremely radical, it is so *within a positivist framework*. That framework sets limits on Labov's advocacy, and without underestimating the usefulness and sincerity of what he says and what he has done, we have to add that in our view the limits of positivism are severe and restrictive.

Labov's positivism is clearly visible in his uneasy juxtaposition of 'objectivity' and 'commitment'. Obviously he is worried that a researcher's advocacy might undermine the validity of her findings (the 'bias' or 'pseudoscience' problem). He gets around the problem by claiming that in this instance, the one reinforced or enhanced the other. It was the work of African American linguists, many motivated at least partly by social and political considerations, that resolved the disagreements, anomalies, distortions and errors of previous work on AVBE. The field became better, more objective and more scientific as a result of these linguists' commitment.

This is a powerful and effective argument if one is inclined to place emphasis on notions of factual truth, error, bias, etc. – in other words, it is a positivistic argument. For a non-positivist it concedes too much – the absolute fact/value distinction for example, and the notion that there is one true account that we will ultimately be able to agree on. It is not the political sensitivity but the more detailed knowledge of the African American linguists, not their values but their facts that Labov implicitly credits here. The argument that there is some intrinsic connection between one's facts and one's values (see above) would presumably fail to impress him.

In the course of his argument, Labov also begs some vital questions: for instance, does a shared racial origin reduce the division between researcher and researched to the point of insignificance? What is the researcher, African American or not, to do if the community contains differing interests and opinions within itself (as is actually the case, if not in Ann Arbor then certainly in the African American community as a whole on the question of AVBE)?

The point here is that Labov's account advises advocate researchers to take an auxiliary role, but in practice it leaves them with some very significant powers: the power to identify the 'community' whose interests they will speak for, and the power to decide on an objective truth which they will speak. By alluding to the African American linguists' insider knowledge rather than their political interests, Labov, as we have noted, glosses over the anti-positivist argument that observation is theory-laden and observers bring their values and interests to it. Yet taken seriously, that argument would threaten the basis for Labov's idea of advocacy: that advocates pay their debt to the community by countering error and bias with the objective factual truth to which their expert status gives them privileged access.

In this connection we also have questions about the idea of 'expert testimony', since it accepts a radical, qualitative distinction between 'our' expert knowledge and 'their' lay knowledge (with the African American linguists standing rather uneasily on the border between us and them) that may in fact be a mystification. If expert knowledge depends on the knowledge of the researched (albeit expressed more technically and systematically) then there is something wrong with presenting it as more different and special than it is (though we do not want to imply here that there is *nothing* special about expert knowledge: technicality and systematicity have important virtues. It is mystification of what makes knowledge 'expert' that we argue against).

We are also, of course, aware that it would be stupid and damaging for experts to stop giving evidence tomorrow on the grounds that their knowledge is no more authentic than the knowledge of those on whose behalf they are speaking. Nevertheless we do not think it naïve to put to such experts the following question: is speaking for people enough? For one could ask why, if experts are under an obligation to defend the powerless, they should not be under the further obligation to empower them to defend themselves.

Empowerment

So far we have spoken of 'empowerment' and 'empowering research' as if the meaning of those expressions were self-evident. It will surprise no-one if we now admit that they are not transparent or straightforward terms. As soon as we have dealt with the positivist objection that 'empowering research' is biased and invalid, we are likely to face more sophisticated questions from more radical quarters, in particular, 'what do you mean by power and what is empowerment?', followed swiftly by 'and how do you know who needs or wants to be "empowered"?'. We regard those questions as entirely justified, and we will attempt to address them now.

Power

Philosophical analyses of power dwell on two aspects: its genesis and its scope. So philosophers ask whether Mao was right to say that 'power proceeds from the barrel of a gun' or if Marx was right that the class with economic power also enjoys cultural and political power. Debates have raged over whether power is 'the ability to get something done', as Bertrand Russell said; or whether the concept only applies to cases where 'some persons can produce intended or foreseen effects on others', as Dennis Wrong insists. There are arguments about whether power has to be something intentional: Steven Lukes, for instance, has suggested that power effects can be produced without necessarily being consciously intended. Take the example of a factory owner who pollutes a river – there may be no intentional pressure on the local people to refrain from protesting, but if the owner dominates the economy and employs many people the effect may be to silence protest, and even if unintended this is an effect of power. And there are also arguments about whether one can say power is being exercised over someone even if they put up no resistance.[4]

The writers cited above may not agree completely on their definition of 'power', but all of them treat it as the sort of thing individuals and groups can have more or less of, or which is more or less equally distributed. Metaphorically, they are positing an *economy* of power. In this 'economic' framework, the term 'empowering' fits quite easily: it entails that people can acquire or be given more power than they currently have, just as they could acquire or be given more money or more goods.

But this way of thinking about power has been fiercely challenged by Michel Foucault, who is opposed to monolithic concepts like those of Marx and Mao. Although we are aware that Foucault's thought is complex and hard to pin down – he purposely made it so to avoid being read in reductive and authoritarian ways – we will try to clarify the point of his objection.

For Foucault, the proposition that power emanates from gun barrels or from economic ownership, and the obvious implication that if we want to know who in society is powerful we should look for those who hold the guns, or own the factories, is hopelessly simplistic and positivist. It implies that power is an intentional product which is then exercised or employed, and Foucault insists this is the wrong picture. On the other hand, he would not be happy with Lukes's idea of unintended power effects either, because it still implies a division of people or groups into 'powerful' and 'powerless', with the further implication that the powerless could wrest power from the powerful.

Power, in Foucault's view, is just not this kind of 'thing': rather it is a force and an effect which exists and circulates in a web of social interaction:

> Power is employed and exercised through a net-like organisation. And not only do individuals circulate between its threads; they are always in the position of simultaneously undergoing and exercising this power. They are not only its inert or consenting target; they are always also the elements of its articulation. In other words, individuals are the vehicles of power, not its point of application.
>
> (Foucault 1980: 98)

The implication of this rather dense passage is that Foucault does not want to see power as something individual human agents create, have or use, but as something that exists prior to them and works through them.

The theme of Foucault's historical work is how power is organised and manifested through knowledge (see the earlier section on Power/ Knowledge, pp. 2–5) and through practices like surveillance, imprisonment, classifying people as mad, defining sexuality and sexual deviance, and so forth. These practices do function in the interests of the bourgeoisie. Nevertheless it would be simplistic to see the bourgeoisie as 'powerful' oppressors and the proletariat as 'powerless' victims, because power is not monolithic and does not go in one direction only. The process of 'power/knowledge' that brings into existence 'the criminal classes' equally brings into existence the threat they pose to bourgeois society; the definition of a group of people as 'homosexuals', a category of sexual deviants, gives those same people a clear identity on the basis of which they can organise for what are now well-known as 'gay rights'. In other words, there is no power without resistance. Power engenders resistance and is always being resisted.

The point that power is not monolithic – that is, it does not emanate from one fundamental source such as the barrel of a gun or the ownership of the means of production – is important to Foucault with his metaphor of the 'net-like organisation', but it has also been echoed by many other contemporary theorists (large numbers of feminists, for example). More and more, such theorists are insisting that there are many simultaneous dimensions of power – for instance class, race, ethnicity, gender, generation, sexuality, subculture – and that theories which privilege one dimension (most commonly, class) as the 'ultimate' source of power are inadequate to capture the complexities of social relations.

Our own position on power draws on both Foucaultian and non-Foucaultian understandings. We do treat power metaphorically as a property which some people in some contexts can have more of than others – that is, we cannot follow Foucault all the way in his rejection of the 'economic' metaphor. On the other hand we follow him in understanding it as a multiple relation (not something that has a single source, as in marxism or maoism); in emphasising its connection with knowledge and 'regimes of truth'; and in recognising the links between power and resistance.

Our decision to retain some notion of people or groups being more or less powerful exposes us to a further challenge, however. A sceptic might well ask how the would-be empowering researcher recognises who has more and who has less power: are we implying that the powerful and the powerless are recognisable to researchers as the poor and the wealthy are recognisable to economists? Obviously, if we were marxists or maoists who took economic ownership or gun holding as straightforward indicators of power we could answer 'yes' to the sceptic's question. Since we have already said we find these views simplistic we are obliged to answer more thoughtfully. For if the 'real' centre of power is impossible to locate and we cannot identify who has power and who has not, how can we talk blithely about 'empowering research' as if it were easy to see where power lies and to alter its distribution?

We think this question lends weight to our argument that people's own definitions and experiences have to be considered. But consulting those involved, though it tells us something about how they perceive the question of power, does not automatically solve the problem: once again, we encounter the issue we discussed in relation to ethnomethodology, whether the actor's subjective account is the ultimate or only truth. Is, say, the happy slave's account of her experience the final account of it? To that we have to respond that the spectre of moral relativism is a frightening one. We would not want to be in a position where we could not assert, for instance, that slavery is wrong, or that extremes of wealth and poverty are unjust and undesirable.

The sceptic who thinks our notion of power simplistic, and challenges us to identify these 'powerless' people whom we propose to empower, has perhaps oversimplified the notion of empowerment. We must return here to the principle that power is not monolithic – the population does not divide neatly into two groups, the powerful and the powerless – from which it follows that 'empowering' cannot be a simple matter of transferring power from one group to the other, or giving people power when before they had none. Precisely because power operates across so many social divisions, any individual must have a complex and multiple identity: the person becomes an intricate mosaic of differing power potentials in different social relations. And we should not forget a further complication, that those who are dominated in particular social relations can and do develop powerful oppositional discourses of resistance – feminism, Black power, gay pride, for example – to which, again, people respond in complex ways. Importantly, though, the extent to which oppositional discourses and groupings are organised or alternative meanings generated varies: some groups are more cohesive and more effective in resistance than others.

Seeing power in these more complex and contextual terms might absolve us from the need to identify some fixed and static group of powerless people, but obviously it imposes upon us the obligation to be attentive to the complexities of power in situations into which we might be researching. One can point to many examples of research where the dynamics of power were oversimplified with regrettable consequences. Among the most notorious are those aid and development projects which, in trying to empower a 'third world' community in the context of the global economy, have unwittingly shifted resources from the community's women to the men, thus reinforcing (or in some cases arguably introducing) a hierarchy of gender. Conceptualising empowerment in terms of 'the community', researchers in such cases failed to see that the community itself contained differing interests and was a site of power relations. (This incidentally is a good example of observation being theory-laden: it took feminist economists to notice and point out the implicit sexism.)

Another somewhat tricky question concerns those instances where relatively powerless people (on one dimension) are nevertheless oppressing others (on a different dimension): racist factory workers, schoolteachers, working-class men. Or there are cases where extreme privilege and some degree of oppression apparently coexist, as with the upper-class public schoolgirls in Frazer's research (chapter Four). What do we think about the project of empowering subjects like these? Are there groups of people (stockbrokers? rapists? National Front supporters?) for whom only the most distant and objectifying research methods would be appropriate, or do we owe it to all human beings, however repellent we find them, to interact with them as persons and take on their agendas?

Although these extreme cases did not arise concretely in our research (and as we have said already, it is difficult even to get research access to those powerful elites who might test the principle to its limits), all of us encountered the problem in a less extreme form (the snobbish and racist public schoolgirl, the Panjabi–English bilingual who makes disparaging remarks about Bangladeshis, the *campesino* who beats his partner). We found ourselves grappling not with absolutes (power, powerlessness) but with the complex positionings of real individuals (including, of course, ourselves). In addressing the question of who 'has power' and who needs or merits 'empowerment' there is a balance to be negotiated between on

21

one hand the understandings of the researched and on the other the political perceptions of the researcher. Dialogue, explicitness and honesty are required if that negotiation is to take place.

EMPOWERING RESEARCH

Having addressed – though not resolved – the difficulties of defining and locating power, we must now turn our attention to the more specific question of what is meant by 'empowering research'. Since that in effect is the overall theme of this book, we would prefer at this stage to speak rather provisionally: what we offer, therefore, is a working definition, together with some observations and questions that will be taken up again in the case histories and the conclusion.

We have characterised 'ethical research' as *research on* and 'advocacy research' as *research on and for*. We understand 'empowering research' as *research on, for and with*. One of the things we take that additional 'with' to imply is the use of interactive or dialogic research methods, as opposed to the distancing or objectifying strategies positivists are constrained to use. It is the centrality of interaction 'with' the researched that enables research to be empowering in our sense; though we understand this as a necessary rather than a sufficient condition.

We should also point out that we do not think of empowerment as an absolute requirement on all research projects. (As we noted in our discussion of power and power relations, there are instances where one would not wish to empower research subjects: though arguably there is political value in researching on powerful groups, such an enterprise might well be one instance where 'research on' would be the more appropriate model.) But if we are going to raise the possibility of 'research on, for and with' as an appropriate goal in some contexts, we must also acknowledge that the standards and constraints of positivist 'research on' – objectivity, disinterestedness, non-interaction – will not be appropriate in those contexts. This raises the question: what alternative standards would be appropriate?

Whatever standards we propose at this stage can only be provisional: much more discussion is needed. In the introduction we will simply raise – without saying too much about the difficulties – a number of points that struck us as key issues when we began the discussions that led to this book. They are issues that will come up repeatedly in the following chapters, and it needs to be borne in mind that each case study will inevitably modify whatever position we seem to be taking up here. In writing this book, as in our research itself, we did not always finish in the same place we started from: the question of where we ended up must be deferred for the conclusion.

The three main issues we will take up in this provisional way are (a) the use of interactive methods; (b) the importance of subjects' own agendas; and (c) the question of 'feedback' and sharing knowledge. On each of these points we will begin with a programmatic statement and then pose various questions in relation to it. Throughout the discussion we will bear in mind our working definition of empowering research as 'research on, for and with'.

(a) 'Persons are not objects and should not be treated as objects.'

The point of this statement is not one that needs to be laboured, since we believe most researchers would find it wholly uncontentious that persons are not objects, and are entitled to respectful treatment. What is more contentious is how strictly we define 'treating persons as objects', and whether if we make the definition a strict one we can avoid objectification and still do good ('valid') research.

We have raised the question of whether 'ethical research' permits methods (e.g. concealment of the researcher's purpose) that might be regarded as objectifying. Indeed, we have asked whether non-interactive methods are by definition objectifying, and thus inappropriate for empowering research. If empowering research is research done 'with' subjects as well as 'on' them it must seek their active co-operation, which requires disclosure of the researcher's goals, assumptions and procedures.

On the question of whether this kind of openness undermines the quality or validity of the research, it will already be clear what we are suggesting. We have devoted a great deal of space in this chapter to the argument that interaction *enhances* our understanding of what we observe, while the claims made for non-interaction as a guarantee of objectivity and validity are philosophically naïve.

The question before us, then, is how we can make our research methods more open, interactive and dialogic. This is not a simple matter, particularly in situations of inequality: but it is one to which we will pay close attention in the case studies presented in the next four chapters.

(b) 'Subjects have their own agendas and research should try to address them.'

One of the ways in which researchers are powerful is that they set the agenda for any given project: what it will be about, what activities it will involve, and so on. But from our insistence that 'persons are not objects' it obviously follows that researched persons may have agendas of their own, things they would like the researcher to address. If we are researching 'with' them as well as 'on and for' them, do we have a responsibility to acknowledge their agendas and deal with them in addition to our own?

This might involve only fairly minor adjustments to research procedures: making it clear, for instance, that asking questions and introducing topics is not the sole prerogative of the researcher. While
traditional handbooks for positivist research warn against addressing
questions subjects might ask (a difficult instruction to follow, as Ann
Oakley has noted, see Frazer's discussion in chapter 4), interactive
methods oblige the researcher not only to listen but also, if called upon,
to respond. But making space for subjects' agendas might mean rather
more than this. It might mean allowing the researched to select a focus
for joint work, or serving as a resource or facilitator for research they
undertake themselves. There are obvious similarities here with the
tradition of 'action research', or with the work of Alain Touraine (again,
discussed in Frazer's chapter).

In the case studies which follow, we discuss in concrete terms how
researchers can respond more fully to the concerns of the researched
(without, however, losing sight of their own concerns); and we also raise
the question whether this proceeding too might enhance the quality of a
research project overall. Activities that are 'added on' in order to meet
subjects' needs may turn out to generate new insights into the activities
the researcher defined: in other words, 'our' agenda and 'theirs' may
sometimes intertwine.

(c) 'If knowledge is worth having, it is worth sharing.'

This is perhaps the most complicated of the issues we are raising here. Is
it, or should it be, part of the researcher's brief to 'empower' people in
an educational sense, by giving them access to expert knowledge,
including the knowledge a research project itself has generated?

First, let us backtrack: what is this 'expert knowledge'? For, to a very
substantial degree, social researchers' knowledge is and must be constructed out of subjects' own knowledge; if this is made explicit (as
arguably it should be) the effect might be to demystify 'expert knowledge' as a category. Such a blurring of the boundary between what 'we'
know and what 'they' know, brought about by making explicit the
processes whereby knowledge acquires its authority and prestige, might
itself be empowering. But it does complicate the picture of 'sharing
knowledge', suggesting that there are different sorts of knowledge to be
shared and different ways of sharing.

To make this clearer, it is helpful to draw a couple of brief examples
from the case studies. Ben Rampton (chapter 2) and Deborah Cameron
(chapter 5) chose to share with their informants some fairly straightforward facts – one might say, 'content knowledge' – about the history of
English in the Indian subcontinent and in the Caribbean respectively.
They found the young people they were working with had been
misinformed, or not informed, about the historical background to the

varieties they spoke, and they tried to fill this gap. Harvey's (chapter 3) discussion of such issues with her Peruvian informants was more informal, given that they did not unambiguously identify her as an expert on the nature of their discursive practices. Rather less straightforwardly, Elizabeth Frazer (chapter 4) used a technique of getting girls to analyse a transcript of their own previous interaction. What she offered was not factual or content knowledge, but an insight into the *process* whereby a researcher examines and draws meaning from informants' discourse – as it were, into the construction of (academic) knowledge.

Although Frazer did something different from the others, in each of these cases the researcher intervened to make available to subjects an alternative interpretation of their beliefs, attitudes or behaviour. In effect, they were taking what subjects had said or done and responding, using skills that are developed in academic training and in teaching, 'you could also look at it this way'. Obviously this did not guarantee that the informants took up the alternative understanding offered them. But most research, even when it is precisely concerned with finding out what subjects think, does not provide opportunities for this kind of reinterpretation. Indeed, for the positivist researcher such intervention would be anathema, since a cardinal rule is to leave your subjects' beliefs as far as possible undisturbed.

Needless to say, we are not greatly upset if our practice separates us from positivist researchers. But it might also seem to separate us from the many researchers who, sincerely and properly concerned about the imbalance of power between themselves and their subjects, follow the apparently very different practice of 'letting subjects speak for themselves'. There is a convention in some contemporary research of reproducing subjects' own words on the page unmediated by authorial comment, in order to give the subject a voice of her own and validate her opinions. This *non*-intervention might also be claimed as an empowering move.[5]

In assessing these two strategies, intervention versus 'giving a voice', one might want to distinguish between what is empowering in the context of *representing* subjects (that is, in a text such as an article, a book or a film) and what is empowering in the context of *interacting* with them. In the former context we see that there may be value in non-intervention (though see Bhavnani (1988), who criticises some instances for perpetuating stereotypes and reproducing disinformation). But in the latter context we have our doubts whether subjects are most empowered by a principled refusal to intervene in their discourse. Discourse after all is a historical construct: whether or not intervention changes someone's opinions, it is arguable that they gain by knowing where those opinions have 'come from' and how they might be challenged or more powerfully formulated. Clearly, it is a principle we use when we teach: not only do we engage with students' views, we engage with them *critically*. The question we are raising, then, is whether there is some merit in extending that practice from the context of the classroom to the context of research.

Even if we decide to answer this question in the affirmative (a matter to be explored further in the individual case studies), other questions remain as to how knowledge can be shared, and what the effects might be. There is also the question of how to integrate educational or knowledge-sharing aims into the broader scope of a research project. Again, this is most helpfully framed by examining specific cases in which we tried, with varying success, to do it.

The case studies

We have now gone as far as we can with the general discussion of these questions, and must turn to a more concrete and more fully contextual-ised discussion: in short, to examples of actual research in all its complexity. Once again, we would emphasise that our own research, the research we will present in the next four chapters, has not always met the standard of our working definition: the case studies are not models for empowering research. After all, none of us undertook our projects as feasibility studies for particular methods; like most researchers we did not focus on method as an end in itself, but rather as a means to solve the problems our projects addressed. For some of us, as the case studies make clear, differing methods and epistemologies coexisted in the same piece of research. The distinct positions we have laid out here are constructs that emerged in retrospect, and their neatness and clarity on the page is a far cry indeed from the muddle and messiness of the actual research experience from which we later abstracted them.

Acknowledging our earlier point that the researcher is also a socially located person, not remote and disembodied but present in the scene, we have chosen to present our case studies as first-person narratives (the 'I' of the narrative is named and credited with authorship of the relevant chapter). And it is very important to bear in mind that the 'I' is different in each case. Although all of us assess our projects in terms of the common framework we have developed in this introduction, the original orientation of each researcher was quite distinctive; we were asking different questions about language and language use.

One point that is worth making in this connection is that 'language' is defined in a number of different ways in our case studies. This reflects the way particular disciplines approach language: someone trained as a linguist will tend to look at language data in one way while a sociologist will look at it in another. Thus 'language' in this volume will sometimes primarily refer to an order of *meaning* – what some social theorists would gloss as 'discourse', while at other times it will refer to a formal system – what some linguistic theorists would gloss as 'grammar'.[6] Which definition is foregrounded in any particular case depends very much on the aims of the study.

In chapter 2 Ben Rampton presents his sociolinguistic research into language use and language attitudes among Asian boys in an English town. Working with both variationist sociolinguistics and the ethnography of communication, he looked at the distribution of syntactic and phonetic variables and their social significance for speakers and for educators. Penelope Harvey in chapter 3 discusses an anthropological study of language use among bilinguals in the southern Peruvian Andes, looking particularly at the role of language in the construction and maintenance of social hierarchy within the peasant culture of a postcolonial state. Elizabeth Frazer's broadly sociological research, examined in chapter 4, addresses the construction of gender, race and class identities among British teenage girls from different socioeconomic backgrounds. Her project centred on the way language use, the girls' talk about themselves, related to their experience of themselves. Finally, in chapter 5 Deborah Cameron analyses a project on language and racism which she carried out with members of a youth club in London, eventually producing a video which explored the topics of verbal racism and Afro-Caribbean linguistic heritage.

In the conclusion, we will return to some of the questions these four research projects raise, both individually and when contrasted with one another. We will ask how our different aims affected our methods and how they constrained or enhanced the possibilities for empowerment. Using this comparative approach, we will also consider more generally what kinds of research questions can be addressed effectively through research 'on, for and with', and what might make it either desirable or undesirable for a linguistic researcher to use empowering research methods in a given situation.

NOTES

1 For more detailed (but accessible) treatment of the philosophy of science and of the three positions discussed here see Chalmers 1982, Outhwaite 1987, Ryan 1970, Trigg 1985.

2 An interesting argument could be made that quantitative sociolinguistics has tendencies towards realism, because in some versions it treats observable variation as the effect of a probabilistic component in speakers' grammars, which in turn are held to be 'real' (obviously there are connections here with the debate in general linguistic theory on the status and 'psychological reality' of grammar). As regards *methodology* however, and particularly as regards the definition of good data and satisfactory data collection, quantitative sociolinguistics is united and unashamedly positivist.

3 This debate is presented clearly in Hollis and Lukes (eds) 1982.
4 Two useful books on philosophical questions relating to power are Lukes 1974 and Lukes 1986.
5 Though see Harvey (chapter 3) for a critical discussion of this issue.
6 We are here using the term 'grammar' in its linguistic sense, referring not just to syntax (word order), but including also phonology and morphology.

2

SCOPE FOR EMPOWERMENT
IN SOCIOLINGUISTICS?

M. B. H. Rampton

Perhaps it is often only while you are doing a piece of research that you actually find out the kind of research that you would ideally like to do. This certainly seems to be quite frequently the case in Ph.D. research, and as a result, quite a good deal of effort can be spent back-pedalling, trying to reshape what you've done to fit changing ideas of what it is that you want.

It may be in this process of reformulation that the relevance of this chapter lies. The study it describes does not illustrate the emergence of a coherent model of empowering research. But questions about social equity were a concern throughout, and the shift that gradually took place can be connected up to quite large and systematic differences in the way that sociolinguists have approached the relationship between researcher and researched. So as well as providing a case study which may help to give sharper definition to the framework being developed in this book, this chapter tries to clarify some fundamental divergences within sociolinguistics.

I shall begin with a short narrative of my own research project: how I began in the first place, my misgivings once I started, my good luck in keeping fieldwork options open, and the rediscovery of an educational relevance that I had given up for lost. I shall then provide a largely diagrammatic summary of my research findings, together with an account of discussion about them with informants. From that point, I shall turn to consider two dominant strands within sociolinguistics – the variationist sociolinguistics associated with William Labov, and the ethnography of communication associated with Dell Hymes. How do their approaches to the relationship between the researcher–researched differ, how did my own research project decide between them, and what are the links to our analytic framework and the distinctions between ethical, advocate and empowering research?

SETTING OUT AND DOING THE RESEARCH

Before I started the research, I was employed as a teacher of English as a second language (ESL) in the south Midlands in the late 1970s. At one of the institutions where I worked, I was put in charge of a group of 9-year-olds of Indian and Pakistani descent who had been born and educated in England. They were being completely withdrawn from mainstream schools and placed in a language centre alongside pupils who had just arrived from overseas. In fact, these youngsters spoke extremely fluent English: their most obvious difficulties were in reading, and if they had been white, they would have certainly been given extra help in their ordinary schools. But because their parents came originally from South Asia, it was commonly assumed that instruction in an ESL Centre would be most appropriate for them.

In other parts of the country the error in this kind of practice was already being discussed[1] and I had no doubts that a mistake had been made. But I was also aware that educational rationales were available which could make this kind of segregation seem acceptable. In particular, it was frequently proposed by researchers and educationalists that pupils of South Asian extraction were very likely to have rather subtle flaws in their English, that their fluency was frequently 'superficial' and 'deceptive', and that specialist language teaching was needed well beyond the initial stages.[2] It would be useful if the flaws in this 'regime of truth' could be shown up once and for all, and this seemed to be a worthwhile purpose for research.

At the time, highly influential applied sociolinguistic work was being produced in Britain arguing that the language of pupils of Afro-Caribbean descent was systematic, and that teachers should treat it with respect rather than regard it as just 'broken English' (e.g. Edwards 1979; Sutcliffe 1982). The same case was being made for white speakers of non-standard English (Trudgill 1975) and it seemed obvious that the argument could be usefully extended to Asian pupils. What was being called ESL and deceptive fluency could in fact be a (new) non-standard Asian dialect of English: if this was the case, then it would be just as easy to question specialist ESL withdrawal for Asian pupils as it would be to challenge special 'remedial' teaching for white Anglo and Afro-Caribbean speakers of non-standard English. So I set out to look for a new dialect of Asian English.

In this initial formulation of what I planned to do, the connections between academic knowledge and educational and social influence seemed plain. But quite rapidly, the value of this direction became less clear. As originally framed, the research would involve the correction of common educational misconceptions and advocacy on behalf of Asian pupils ('look how these dialectalisms are being mistreated as mistakes:

see how grammatically consistent they are'). But around that time in circles associated with the study of education (as elsewhere), the intellectual climate discouraged any view that research was unproblematically objective. Research by white on black came in for as much scrutiny as any other (cf. e.g. Alladina 1986; Hobsbaum 1982; Jones 1988), and in this context it was unsurprising that I should start to wonder about the validity and implications of my setting out to define a 'British Asian English'. The designation of varieties and dialects is after all quite arbitrary – how many distinctive linguistic features are needed to warrant a special label? And even then, is it really justified to launch an 'Asian English Vernacular' onto the public stage when, let's say, it differs from white vernaculars in 20 linguistic items and resembles them in 2,200? Linguists might well understand the ground rules for such short-hand idealisation, but there is no reason why others should. And in a context where a web of social factors leads to discrimination and stereotypes about deviation, there seemed to be few grounds for assuming that educational integration would necessarily follow on from a demonstration that non-standard Asian Englishes were grammatically systematic. Even though it has often been argued that language is legitimate where it is systematic (e.g. Labov 1969), there is no necessary connection between legitimacy and system: few people would, I imagine, want to argue that crime is acceptable in those cases where it is organised. Explanation and justification aren't the same.

Faced with these realisations, I drew back from the idea that my empirical work should have direct educational relevance (I wrote some critiques of educational orthodoxy, but didn't link these to particularly extensive analyses of language use – cf. Rampton 1983, 1985). Without expecting that it would have any practical spin off, I decided to pursue a topic that would have its central relevance within an academic frame of reference. Engaging with quite recent British developments in variationist sociolinguistics (especially Le Page 1980; Milroy 1980), I took an interest in the idea of speaker identity, and decided to look at the connection between two aspects of pronunciation and the extent to which these were influenced by the people with whom a speaker associated interactively, and the people with whom they identified psychologically (cf. e.g. Rampton 1989). This concern was consistent with the doubts that I now had about my earlier plans, where I would have run a serious risk of simply substituting new stereotypes for old. In my revised plan, instead of simply describing a category, I was addressing the principles of classification themselves, and I was moving beyond biological definitions to an analysis that recognised flexibility and multiplicity as central features of group membership. But nothing of immediate social or educational relevance was expected.

I began fieldwork in 1984 in the neighbourhood where I had been working as a teacher and youth worker from 1978–80. From the outset I made it plain that I was interested in language and the way it fitted in with young people's social life, and my hybrid field role was made up of at least three components. In part I was an ex-teacher, who had access to local schools and knew a lot of the teachers. This merged quite easily with a position as youth worker: I organised trips to sporting events, spent a lot of time on holiday play schemes and in the local youth club, and was addressed by my first name. Third, I was a student doing a project on language (so that, for example, on one occasion, an informant told a friend to be more serious in an interview 'because we want Ben to pass'). My contacts with informants were largely limited to more organised areas of peer group recreation and to the more informal parts of the school day (lunchtimes and breaktimes, though I also conducted a substantial number of interviews in a separate room during lesson times). In the end I collected data on an extended friendship network of twenty-three 11- to 14-year-old boys of Afro-Caribbean, white Anglo, Indian and Pakistani descent (numbering three, three, seven, and ten respectively). I did not include girls, partly because very few attended out-of-school recreational arenas and partly because of the statistical analysis which I had initially planned.

In other respects, however, my fieldwork schedule was broadly drawn. One half followed a preset programme designed to produce quantitative correlations between social, psychological and linguistic variables, using data obtained through interviews and questionnaires. But the other half was more open-ended, leaving space for lines of enquiry to develop more inductively – here the methodology entailed interviews about language, participant observation in a youth club, and radio-microphone recording.

In the course of this more open data collection, I started to come across some language practices, anecdotes and attitudes which all converged towards my earlier concern with the classification of Asian youngsters as ESL learners. This was not a case of observing imperfections in the speech of my informants, who were all highly proficient speakers of English. Instead it involved comments about the ESL centre where I had worked, remarks on the proficiency of a range of people in the neighbourhood, and stylised speech performances in which speakers pretended that they did not know much English. Rather than actually instancing the English competence of Asians, in different ways these appeared to represent an on-going debate about the idea of Asian English itself.

After fourteen months of fairly intensive fieldwork, I withdrew to write up my Ph.D.. I completed the variationist project, and also produced a broadly ethnographic account of the ways in which the multiracial peer group showed an active concern with ESL. During this time, a grant application for further sociolinguistic research in the neighbourhood was successful, and before this second period of field-work began, I produced a diagrammatic summary of my Ph.D. findings, which I then discussed with my former informants in 1987–88 (in the following visual display Part C describes the variationist project, Parts A and B the ethnography).

It will help to clarify the unanticipated relevance which emerged through open-ended investigation if I present these diagrams here, along with one or two very brief notes of explanation. It will also provide a context for some comments on the ways in which these diagrams were discussed with informants. In their presentation here, they are rather bare and fall somewhat short of the precision normally required in scholarly description. But they give an overall picture, and more importantly, represent the kind of account that I thought would be accessible to the particular audience that I had in mind (much fuller argument and methodological discussion can be found in Rampton 1987, 1988, 1989).

THE RESEARCH FINDINGS

The visual display of these results falls into three main sections:

Part A: Different arenas of adolescent social life
Part B: How the English language fits in with these four domains
Part C: Language and belonging to social groups

The data for Part C and part of Part A were obtained by means of the elicitation programme planned in advance, quantitative comparison being the final objective. The rest of Part A and most of Part B emerged through the more open-ended methods. For discussion purposes, the following diagrams were greatly enlarged, and the questions and answers outlined in Part C were photocopied. The visual presentation in Part B may not be competely clear to the reader, and so the Appendix contains a prose summary written at the same time, which captures some of the main points I was trying to make in oral discussion.

An outline of the description of language in one part of Exhampton contained in my thesis 'Uses of English in a multilingual British peer group'

Part A: Different arenas in adolescent social life

During the week, young people move around different places, they meet different people and they do different things. But there are patterns in all this.

Diagram 1 Four domains for boys in Exhampton, with the settings and activities which I think go with each

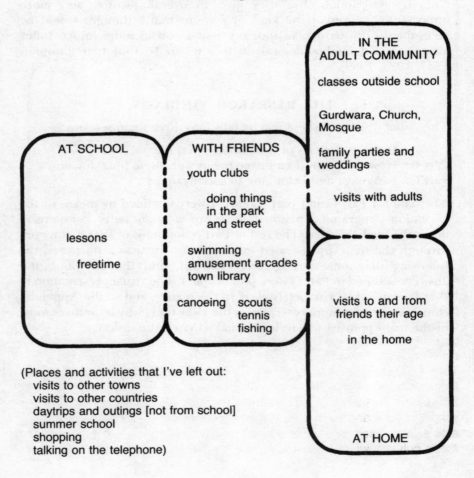

AT SCHOOL

lessons

freetime

WITH FRIENDS

youth clubs

doing things in the park and street

swimming
amusement arcades
town library

canoeing   scouts
            tennis
            fishing

IN THE ADULT COMMUNITY

classes outside school

Gurdwara, Church, Mosque

family parties and weddings

visits with adults

visits to and from friends their age

in the home

AT HOME

(Places and activities that I've left out:
   visits to other towns
   visits to other countries
   daytrips and outings [not from school]
   summer school
   shopping
   talking on the telephone)

Diagram 2   Some of the different things that happen in these domains

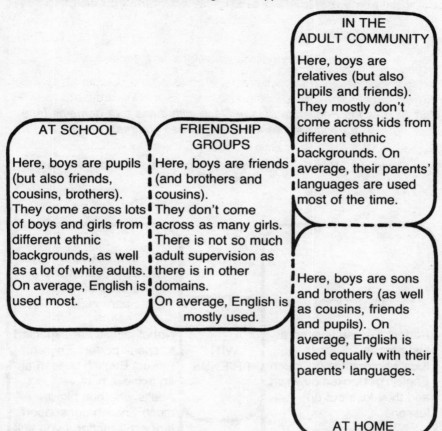

IN THE ADULT COMMUNITY

Here, boys are relatives (but also pupils and friends). They mostly don't come across kids from different ethnic backgrounds. On average, their parents' languages are used most of the time.

AT SCHOOL

Here, boys are pupils (but also friends, cousins, brothers). They come across lots of boys and girls from different ethnic backgrounds, as well as a lot of white adults. On average, English is used most.

FRIENDSHIP GROUPS

Here, boys are friends (and brothers and cousins). They don't come across as many girls. There is not so much adult supervision as there is in other domains. On average, English is mostly used.

Here, boys are sons and brothers (as well as cousins, friends and pupils). On average, English is used equally with their parents' languages.

AT HOME

A note on Diagrams 1 and 2:
In the rings on the left (at school), white English (middle class) values predominate. In the rings on the right, the values of kids' parents are dominant. But this diagram is *misleading* if it suggests that there is a big gap between school and home domains: in a variety of ways there is a clear understanding of school both at home and in the adult community. These diagrams are also definitely not intended to suggest that with their friends, young people are somehow '*stranded* between two worlds'. However, I do think that kids do have a combined knowledge of both school culture and their parents' culture which is greater than anyone else's. Also, they have most scope to mix and blend different parts of these cultures when they're with their friends.

35

Part B: How the English language fits in with these four domains (see appendix for an alternative prose summary)

Diagram 3   How English is seen at school, at home and in the adult community

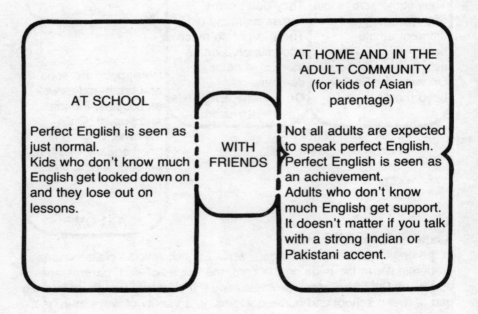

AT SCHOOL

Perfect English is seen as just normal.
Kids who don't know much English get looked down on and they lose out on lessons.

WITH FRIENDS

AT HOME AND IN THE ADULT COMMUNITY
(for kids of Asian parentage)

Not all adults are expected to speak perfect English.
Perfect English is seen as an achievement.
Adults who don't know much English get support.
It doesn't matter if you talk with a strong Indian or Pakistani accent.

Diagram 4   How are these local views of English influenced by the past and by the present national situation?

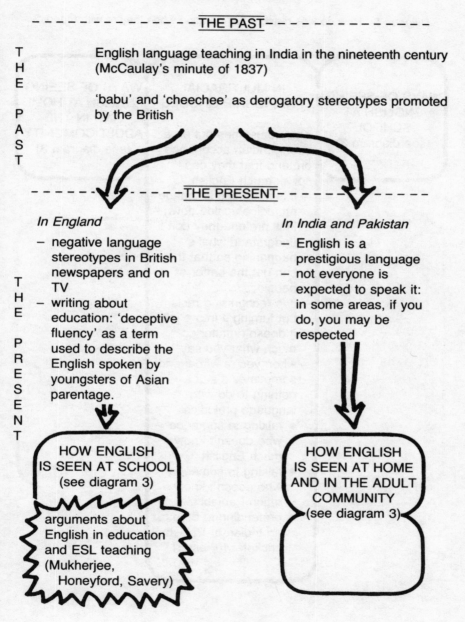

- - - - - - - - - - - - - - -THE PAST- - - - - - - - - - - - - - -

T
H   English language teaching in India in the nineteenth century
E   (McCaulay's minute of 1837)

P   'babu' and 'cheechee' as derogatory stereotypes promoted
A   by the British
S
T

- - - - - - - - - - - - -THE PRESENT- - - - - - - - - - - -

In England

- negative language
  stereotypes in British
  newspapers and on
  TV
- writing about
  education: 'deceptive
  fluency' as a term
  used to describe the
  English spoken by
  youngsters of Asian
  parentage.

In India and Pakistan

- English is a
  prestigious language
- not everyone is
  expected to speak it:
  in some areas, if you
  do, you may be
  respected

T
H
E

P
R
E
S
E
N
T

HOW ENGLISH
IS SEEN AT SCHOOL
(see diagram 3)

HOW ENGLISH
IS SEEN AT HOME
AND IN THE ADULT
COMMUNITY
(see diagram 3)

arguments about
English in education
and ESL teaching
(Mukherjee,
    Honeyford, Savery)

Diagram 5 How do kids react to this situation when they're with friends?

| WAYS OF SEEING ENGLISH AT SCHOOL (see diagram 3) | IN MULTIRACIAL FRIENDSHIP GROUPS | WAYS OF SEEING ENGLISH AT HOME AND IN THE ADULT COMUNITY (see diagram 3) |

IN MULTIRACIAL FRIENDSHIP GROUPS

Kids sometimes put on a strong Indian accent and pretend that they can't speak much English:
- this is turning language prejudice upside down – kids pretend they don't understand what's happening so that they can get the better of people;
- it is recognising racism but turning it into a joke;
- it doesn't matter so much what you say when you're with friends
- sometimes it's got nothing to do with language prejudice
  - talking to someone who doesn't know much English
  - talking to someone who doesn't know much Panjabi
  - pretending to be e.g. an Indian or Pakistani cricketer (or actor).

38

Part C: Language and belonging in social groups

Starting assumptions

There is a link between the way people speak and the social groups that they belong to. A person's language can show what groups they are connected with.

but

LANGUAGE = ? (which *parts* of language show group affiliation?)
BELONGING IN A GROUP = ? (there are many different types of
group and several types of belonging)

for example

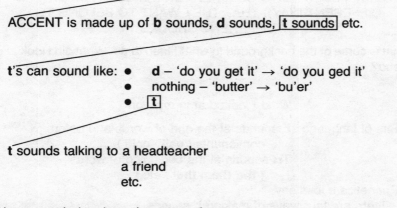

LANGUAGE contains words, grammar, |accent| etc.

ACCENT is made up of **b** sounds, **d** sounds, |t sounds| etc.

t's can sound like: •   d – 'do you get it' → 'do you ged it'
                •   nothing – 'butter' → 'bu'er'
                • |t|

t sounds talking to a headteacher
                       a friend
                       etc.

Also group belonging takes many forms:

GROUP BELONGING:

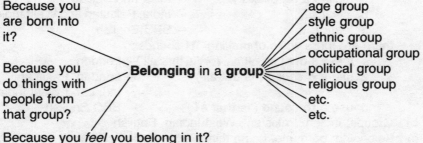

Because you
are born into
it?

Because you
do things with
people from
that group?

Belonging in a **group**

age group
style group
ethnic group
occupational group
political group
religious group
etc.
etc.

Because you *feel* you belong in it?

39

So how does language show what groups you belong in?

Imagine three groups (blue, red and green) and 3 people (A, B and C):
Person A
   born into blue group, goes around with blue group people, and feels he
   belongs in the blue group → talks blue language
Person B
   born into blue group, goes around with blue group people, but feels
   more like a RED group person → talks how?
Person C
   born into blue group, goes around with RED group people, and feels
   more like a GREEN group person → talks how?

d sounds like blue?
g sounds like red?
t sounds like green?
????

THE DIFFERENT BITS OF A PERSON'S SPEECH SHOW THE DIFFERENT WAYS THAT THEY WANT TO BELONG TO DIFFERENT GROUPS

So that is some of the background to what I tried to do. What did I look at in the end?

What I looked at in my work

a) Bits of language: **L** sounds at the end of words and before
                          consonants ('ba**ll**' 'co**l**d')
                      TH sounds at the beginning of words
                          ('**th**e **th**em **th**at', etc.)
    Phonetics books say:
    there are four ways of making **L** sounds
        1 leave it out ('footbore')   – London
        2 make it with the tip of the
           tongue bent back
           (called a retroflex **L**)   – India and Pakistan
        3 'clear **L**'   – India, Pakistan and West Indies
        4 'dark **L**'   – BBC English
    there are three ways of making **TH** sounds
        1 leave it out ('is _at all' for 'is that all')– London
        2 use a **d** sound ('is **d**at all')   – London, Pakistan,
                                            India and West Indies
        3 use a **th** sound ('is **th**at all')   – BBC English
b) Groups: Indian, Pakistani, West Indian, English
c) Belonging: born into, doing things with, feeling similar to

The questions that I asked and the answers that I found

Question 1: Did the country which kids' parents come from, tie up with the way they used **L** and **TH** sounds?

Answer:

mostly no, although it did with one sound.
- everyone used the London style **L** sound some of the time
- everyone used the BBC style **L** some of the time
- nearly everyone used the clear **L** sound a little bit
- everyone dropped the **TH** sound sometimes
- everyone used the BBC **TH** sound quite a lot

but the retroflex **L** sound was different:
- some English kids used the retroflex **L** sound a little, and some Asian kids didn't use it at all, or just a little, but on average, kids with parents who came from India and Pakistan used it more than the others.

Question 2: Did the ethnic background of their close friends tie up with the way kids used **L** and **TH** sounds?

Answer:

No, on five sounds – London style **L**, BBC style **L**, clear **L**,
London **TH**, BBC **TH**

Yes, on two sounds – retroflex **L** and **d** for **TH**
- kids who used more of the retroflex **L** sound had more close friends who were bilingual in English and Panjabi or Urdu. Kids who used that **L** sound less had fewer close friends who could speak Panjabi or Urdu.
- for Indian, English and West Indian kids, having more close Pakistani friends went with using **d** for **TH** more often.

Question 3: Was there a link between the way kids used **L** and **TH** sounds and the ethnic groups that they felt similar to?

Answer:

Mostly no. Most kids didn't think they were much more like one group than another. For example, they didn't think that they were much more like Indian kids than Pakistani, English and West Indian kids. Also, they didn't *want* to be more like one group than another. So most of the time, the way they used **TH** and **L** sounds didn't tie up with the ethnic groups they felt they were similar to.

But there was one connection with retroflex **L**. Pakistani kids who used retroflex **L** most also thought they were most like Pakistani adults. The Pakistani kids who thought they were most different from Pakistani adults made less use of the retroflex **L** sound.

41

DISCUSSION OF THE RESULTS AND
THE RELATIONSHIP BETWEEN RESEARCHER AND
RESEARCHED

During 1987–88, these diagrams were shown to about twenty-five youngsters in small groups of two to five, most of whom had participated in the original study. Parts A and B were always discussed, but after the first couple of presentations, Part C was sometimes dropped if time was running out or if people felt they had had enough. All the sessions were held in a small room in the youth club, and they generally lasted between one and two hours. Attendance was completely voluntary. In a handful of cases, respondents seemed relatively indifferent, but in general, reactions were very positive (thoughtful, animated, interested).

Although by no means routine (cf. AAA 1971 para.1g, BSA 1982 para. 2), research feedback to informants is a fairly common practice in social science, though the purposes and effects are likely to be varied. It obviously brings the investigator's role as a researcher right to the forefront of the relationship with informants, and for this reason some extended consideration of the experience here is relevant to the theme of this book.

In the first place, it is worth clarifying the ways in which I hoped that these feedback sessions would assist my own researching. To quite an extent, these sessions were actually oriented to the post-doctoral research project that I was conducting in 1987–88 (and if I hadn't got funding for this later research, feedback on the earlier project might not have occurred). Guided by the dictates of conscience, I wanted to make sure that before I collected more data, respondents could give consent in a way that was as informed as possible (cf. AAA 1971 para.1b; BSA 1982; Dingwall 1980), and that they had an idea of the kinds of thing that I got up to. Certainly if strong objections had been expressed, the second project would have had to have been substantially revised.

Feeding-back also provided me with information that would be useful when considering publication and dissemination of the research findings. Obviously, a positive response would not abrogate my responsibility as author (cf. Geertz 1988: 140), or provide me with a *carte blanche* to publish anyhow and anywhere. Given my much greater familiarity with the types of reader and context in which the research would be read, in camparison with my informants I remained in a much better position to try to anticipate the effect of what I wrote (an unavoidable obligation, despite its considerable vulnerability). Nevertheless, if in my solitary analysis I had actually worked on a set of locally explosive issues, I would now be likely to find out.

These were the two primary objectives – informed consent and a rough idea of the local impact of what I could be saying. Arguably, these two considerations should override a third benefit that commonly derives from feeding-back results. Beyond simply providing an additional test of validity ('respondent validation': cf. Bloor 1978; Hammersley and Atkinson 1983:195–198), feedback can produce a good deal of further information and refinement for analysis. The risk is that this denies informants the right to break out and stand clear from a research cycle forever incorporating their words and deeds into its pantophagic database: informant reactions to representations of their own lives are absorbed into further representations. In the event, the boys' responses didn't indicate any desire for dissociation from the project and I wasn't forced into a choice between objectives. Had I decided not to tape-record these feedback sessions, commitment to informant autonomy would have been more clearly stated. On the other hand, much valuable (and willing) commentary would have been lost. As it was, the outline of domains, language evaluation, history and code-switching made sense to informants; a good deal of focused supplementary data emerged (e.g. in examples they themselves provided); certain research inferences were contested (e.g. a suggestion that Asian parents were proud of their children's English); and important limitations in the account were underlined (most significantly, a bias in the domains description towards early adolescent boys of Indian and Pakistani parentage).

In part, then, feedback sharpened the content of the research and to quite a degree it was oriented to what we have called ethical aspects of the relationship between researcher and researched (with informants' interests acting as a constraining influence on the investigator's independent plans). But there are grounds for suggesting that its value extended beyond this, and that it offered something to informants in return.

In the first instance, it provided them with information that they either hadn't been aware of or hadn't much attended to. On the whole, informants didn't know about the origins of the babu stereotype and they were unfamiliar with the gist of educational writing about ESL. Beyond that, it made some everyday understandings more explicit. The charting of sociolinguistic domains assisted reflection on the ways in which informants had changed since their early adolescence, and it could be useful in thinking about the ways that life had changed since their grandparents and parents had initially come to Britain. The summary brought together a range of phenomena which informants had been aware of but hadn't necessarily connected. Comic and playful ESL imitations were linked up with attitudes to Asian English at school, at home, in the Indian subcontinent and in the nineteenth century, and this provided leverage on a joking activity (babu impersonation) which was quite widely felt to be politically ambiguous. This also involved recognition of quite uncomfortable contradictions in peer group culture. To some extent, code-switching into stylised Indian English seemed like resistance to racism. But at the same time, it also reiterated it and was commonly used (by informants as well as others) in the racist treatment of another Asian subgroup.[3]

There was also probably some value in the way in which the research gave some recognition and importance to the concerns of these adolescents. I am not suggesting that these informants were locked into private and unacknowledged perceptions and opinions, and that there were no local discourses with which they could interact – it was obvious that there were. Nevertheless, the incorporation of views within 'research knowledge' is likely to feel like a significant ratification, and at least from where I stood, it seemed that this might often be helpful to informants. Their understandings were being shaped within an emergent multiracial youth culture, which lacked the degree of ideological support available to stable, adult and official orders (cf. Hewitt 1986; Rampton 1991). So it might be important that explicit ideologies of multiracial youth community were given some kind of endorsement. Similarly, where informants sensed that it was false to suppose that knowledge of two languages inevitably meant that bilinguals spoke less well than monolinguals, the corroboration offered by a researcher might also be valued.

Of course, up to a point, participant observation, interviewing and ordinary conversation might serve some of these purposes as adequately as systematic feedback. The ratification of personal views is often cited as a reason why people like talking to researchers; interviews and conversations can provide knowledge as well as extract it; they can generate the recognition of hitherto unnoticed connections; and they can highlight contradictions in local practices. To an extent, this happened during fieldwork outside feedback, but it is doubtful whether conversations or interviews can elicit consent that is informed to quite the same extent, and they are unlikely to provide such focused guidance about publication and dissemination. The crucial difference between feedback and discussion during fieldwork relates to the status of the information that the researcher provides.

The information presented in the feedback charts derived from eighteen months of post-fieldwork analysis, working over data on social networks, sociolinguistic attitudes, naturalistic interaction and educational discourse. There was no way in which I could have provided informants with the same kind of systematic and considered account during fieldwork, and there was no way in which I could have pointed out more clearly the special power that I had as a researcher. As Harvey argues (chapter 3), it is when researchers write up their work that the fluid and ambiguous identities encountered during fieldwork become fixed, and it is at this point of public representation that the researcher's authority primarily resides. For these reasons, relatively formal feedback of this kind constitutes a particularly valuable way of making oneself accountable to one's informants.

There is one further point that is worth making about this feedback. As a Ph.D., the synthesis that I presented was carefully organised as a contribution to the public stock of authoritative knowledge to which educationalists, policy-makers, scholars and others might refer (whether or not anyone eventually took any notice is of course another matter). Despite this, the central concepts and arguments in Parts A and B were rapidly grasped by the informants, and in fact this suggested the kinds of ground on which more empowering research could be developed. In these feedback sessions, the distinction between local knowledge as the source of data and academic understanding as the arena for critical discussion, didn't seem to hold in any pure form, and in this there was consistency with aspects of the study's broader thesis. Academic linguistics figured in the empirical field which the research described (seen as supplying/supporting ideas like semilingualism and deceptive fluency), and a central point had been that differently positioned responses to a broadly shared historical inheritance were manifest in the writing of scholars and educationalists on the one hand, and the oblique linguistic play of adolescents on the other. In the accessibility of knowledge which was considered academic enough to get a Ph.D. (as well as forming the basis for a successful application for further research funding), these feedback sessions pointed to the kind of research on language in which it would be possible for informants to take an active role.

This is a point that needs to be elaborated in the next section, where this case study will be linked into some of the arguments about researcher–researched relations that have been expressed in variationist and ethnographic sociolinguistics. But a glance at Part C of the research summary, in which I presented the variationist results, may provide some foretaste.

I have to admit that in presenting Part C to informants, I didn't give it as much of a chance as I might have. It was always presented second, and often accompanied by apologies in case it seemed rather boring. There is no doubt that certain linguistic features in ordinary speech were a matter of some local concern (e.g. the invariant question tag 'innit'), discussion of situational variability was a source of some interest to informants, and when I varied my presentation, so too was the account of multiple group membership. But knowledge from general textbooks might have been as stimulating here as the particular research I did, and the connection between original research and informant clarification seemed less integral than it had before. Rather than being led into it through a range of descriptions which organised ideas that already had local currency, informants were here being rather abruptly presented with a second-order language of analysis, and in general, unreliable though this impression may be, there seemed to be less to provoke them. There also seemed to be much less scope for informants either to correct or to supplement my account.

It is worth now turning to the wider debate about researcher–researched relationships within sociolinguistics. There we may find some larger explanation for the differences in this experience of feeding-back.

RESEARCHER AND RESEARCHED IN SOCIOLINGUISTICS

So far, I have described a shift in the research I did, away from (a) early plans to try to describe 'British Asian English', into (b) a more exclusively academic attempt to correlate speech sounds and multiple group membership, and then, finally, (c) as a result of more open-ended data-collection, into an account of local attitudes to ESL which actually brought me back (in a rather different form) to the issues that I'd started out with. I have also reported the experience of feeding my results back to the informants, and while it was very far from being any kind of controlled experiment, on the basis of this I have suggested that stage (c) produced more relevant and more accessible content. It also contained plainer social, educational and political elements (see Parts A and B).

These developments do not seem accidental if one looks at the disciplinary background to the research. They derive quite systematically from the different types of sociolinguistic tradition with which the work was aligned at different times. This is a point that is worth dwelling on in a little detail, since strong statements have been made about the relationship between researcher and researched by both variationist sociolinguists and by ethnographers of communication.

The educational contribution of sociolinguists working within the variationist paradigm established by William Labov has been very considerable indeed (e.g. Labov 1969; Trudgill 1975). Nevertheless, the relative remoteness and slighter social relevance of the quantitative part of my study (Part C) can, I think, be systematically linked to the influence of the Labovian tradition.[4] This is not primarily a question of the methods of data collection used by variationists, which are highly diverse and often ethnographic (see e.g. Labov 1981; Milroy 1980). The limitations derive from certain central concepts in variationist theory, which prioritise the division of researcher and researched into discrete communities.

In the first place variationists are most interested in one particular type of speech, the 'vernacular':

> Not every (speech) style ... is of equal interest to linguists. Some styles show irregular phonological and grammatical patterns, with a great deal of 'hypercorrection'. In other styles, we find more systematic speech, where the fundamental relations which determine the course of linguistic evolution can be seen most clearly. This is the 'vernacular' – the style in which minimum attention is paid to the monitoring of speech.
>
> (Labov 1972: 208)

This emphasis on the vernacular directs attention away from contact across social groups, even though such contact is regarded as inevitable. Lesley Milroy, for example, is sceptical of the traditional dialectologist's conception of the pure dialect speaker, and of the view that the language of one particular group was in some sense more genuine than that of others (1987: 17). Nevertheless, speech which is most free from the intrusion of prestigious forms is still the most valuable for the linguist (ibid.: 59). Traces of an ideal of 'unmolested' languages, 'one to a community, each working out its own destiny in an autonomous community' (Hymes 1980: 52; see also Gumperz 1982: 26) continue to have some hold (though compare Le Page and Tabouret-Keller 1985).

Interest in the vernacular leads to an emphasis on the 'observer paradox':

> The observer's paradox, which springs from the effects of direct observation upon language, can be characterised as follows: the vernacular is the focus of the linguist's interest, and large volumes of high-quality recordings of speech are needed to describe it. However, since speakers will tend to shift away from their vernaculars in situations where they are being tape-recorded by a stranger, the very act of recording is likely to distort the object of observation.
>
> (Milroy 1987: 59)

The relationship between researcher and researched is clearly a matter of concern. But to a very substantial extent, this is seen as a technical problem, a source of interference to be eliminated – the interaction between researcher and informant is not of itself a matter for investigation.[5] Labov gives the following advice:

> *Power relationships in the interview setting.* One of the crucial elements that determines the course of a sociolinguistic interview and further contacts is the relative degree of authority of the interviewer and speaker. The 'Observer's Paradox' is not to be seen as absolute, but closely linked to the perceived relationship of an outside observer in a dominating class. . . . The interviewer is engaged in an occupation that clearly points to membership in a middle-class institution of some kind – research or journalism. Any

47

identification of the interviewer as a teacher would stress the fact that he is a person that information flows from, not to. The basic counter-strategy of the sociolinguistic interview is to emphasise the position of the interviewer as learner, in a position of lower authority than the person he is talking to.

This favourable interactive position can only be achieved by a thorough-going rejection of the authority that stems from association with the dominating social class. Sociolinguistic interviewers must continually monitor their behaviour for any signs of this authority. They must review their lexical and grammatical choices to remove any evidence of bookishness or influence of literary language, and ruthlessly plane away all remains of conspicuous ostentation to achieve a plain, unvarnished style.

(Labov 1981: 15)

A third characteristic of variationist research emphasises the qualitative difference between judgements of informants and researchers. Mistrust of local language attitudes is implied in the definition of both the observer paradox and the vernacular, where 'attention to speech' is considered obstructive: when informants are aware of language, the data they provide are likely to be impure (Labov 1972: 208). Furthermore, the reports that informants make about their own language use are widely regarded as unreliable (ibid.: 215; Milroy and Milroy 1985: 18). Considerable emphasis is laid upon the difference between the objective facts about language and subjective opinions (e.g. Trudgill and Giles 1978), and priority is given to 'objective facts', to the extent of even suggesting that 'statistical counts of (speech) variants actually used are probably the best way of assessing attitudes' (Milroy and Milroy 1985: 19).[6]

Given specific scholarly objectives, one can argue that these concepts and emphases are practical and productive. Nevertheless, it is plain that all three of these positions discourage dialogue between researcher and researched about the central topics of interest to investigation. The most highly prized data are to be found in zones beyond most researchers' experience; to gain access and avoid the contaminating effect of their own sociolinguistic identities, they should make their approaches only indirectly, concealing their real professional concerns; and although interesting as objects of study, informant attitudes to language do not serve as the stuff of discussion between equals. For researchers seeking sociolinguistic benefit for the communities they investigate, these features of the variationist programme represent substantial obstacles to the development of relatively interactive strategies. They only provide scope for an advocacy role. Indeed, even within advocacy, one can say that they contain certain limitations.

48

Variationist research was highly influential on the issue of linguistic equality during the 1970s and early 1980s. When examined independently of the rules of the standard variety, the vernacular was judged to contain systematic rules of its own. Educational assertions about its inferiority were said to be the result of assessment by the wrong criteria, and the view was taken that, linguistically speaking, nobody's language was worse than anyone else's. This was supplemented by the observer paradox, which suggested error in the linguistic judgement of teachers, and implied that it was only when teachers were not around that pupils showed their real linguistic abilities. As one element in this, there was a romantic and relativistic celebration of 'otherness', more inclined to reject or escape from relations of power than to try to understand them fully. It is now quite widely recognised that the idea of linguistic equality was overstated (cf. Hudson 1983 for a succinct and consensual statement of the difficulties): linguists projected their professional judgements about linguistic structure onto a public stage where people were actually concerned about language use, power relations and ethnic and social identity.[7] Equally, though children often do have a much larger repertoire than they display at school, the judgements of teachers are socially rooted and institutionally unavoidable, and so it is unhelpful simply to dismiss them as wrong.

Indeed more generally one can argue that variationist interventions in public debate about linguistic equality were not assisted by their characteristic suspicion of popular attitudes to language. Negative attitudes to non-standard varieties tended to be treated as prejudice or ignorance of the 'objective facts',[8] and efforts to enter the particular socio-cultural logics in which such attitudes might make sense were customarily restricted to discussions of 'linguistic insecurity', another standardised concept in this tradition (Labov 1972: Wardhaugh 1986). In Britain, it was not altogether surprising to find demagogic counter-reaction, purporting to speak up for common sense against a conspiracy of linguists (Honey 1983).

But it is in Labov's 1982 article on 'Objectivity and commitment in linguistic science', a canonical statement on social responsibility in variationist sociolinguistics (Milroy 1987: 92–93; Trudgill 1984: 3–4) that one can see most clearly the ways in which these tenets constrain social intervention.

The idea of discrete communities seems to run throughout Labov's discussion of the responsibilities of researcher as outsider (1982: 186), and the paper contains only very limited reflection on the overarching relations of knowledge, power and interdependence in which sociolinguistic research on working-class groups is embedded.[9] Labov's central recommendation is that as outsiders, white researchers should give responsibility for political agency and direction to the people inside oppressed communities: they should only look towards instrumental and auxiliary roles for themselves.

At first glance, this seems to be good advice, but a major difficulty remains which Labov passes over rather quickly:

> *It is of course always hard to say who speaks for the community, and finding out the choice of a community forms another whole domain of research.* But for linguists who are studying a speech community that is not their own, like those white linguists who were engaged with the black community, the principle has a clear application. They don't claim for themselves the right to speak for the community or make the decision on what forms of language should be used.
>
> (1982: 186; emphasis added)

This is an important ideal, though Labov himself prefaces it with a major qualification. In fact, the practical difficulties go further, since in actuality, the interconnection of groups in social structure often makes autonomous decision-making impossible. Indeed in the Ann Arbor trial which Labov describes, the final decision about what language should be used at school was taken by a white judge. Labov argues that linguistic intervention in the judicial process gained validity and effectiveness through the participation of black scholars, but he doesn't offer any guidance on the questions that inevitably arise. How was it that black scholars made sure that linguistics took the right path? Plainly, shared biological 'race' is not of itself sufficient to generate a constructive understanding between scholars and local communities (cf. 1982: 178), and even if they come from the localities in question, it is necessary to ask how it is that the long process of graduate initiation and linguistic training presents no threat to their shared experience and interests. Labov argues that black academic representation is a crucial step forward in the emancipation of black communities, but he gives no consideration to the question of social class and the way in which education can change a person's social position and affiliations. Indeed, in its final pages, the paper gives a glimpse of the unresolved difficulties. Throughout, a central place is given to the internal dealings of the academic community, and in rather epic tones, emphasis is laid upon its own infusion with new blood.[10] But there is less confidence about the implications for the social group on whose behalf the legal action was originally taken:

> it isn't clear that effective ways to implement [the trial decision] are on hand, or whether it can make a substantial difference to the education of minority children.
>
> (1982: 194)

One might summarise this by saying that the paper is premised on an analysis of society which is insufficient to its task. It only focuses on a small amount of movement around rather clear-cut boundaries between insiders and outsiders, blacks and whites, researchers and researched; it gives no consideration to social class, to the costs which movement entails, or more generally, to the variable ways in which society links individuals in some capacities while simultaneously dividing them in others. In these weaknesses, again variationist assumptions seem to be in play. The analysis fits with the idea of vernaculars and relatively discrete communities, and is consistent with the methodological recommendation that interviewers should conceal the social origin and character of their interests and try to shift categories, from outside in (see the quotation above from Labov 1981: 15; in contrast, consider the possibility of admitting one's research identity, but building field relationships so that it is only one strand among several).

There are in fact some clear signs in the paper that Labov himself is uneasy with variationist epistemology as a basis for social intervention. He begins with the premise that scientific objectivity and social commitment involve separate activities:

> the application of linguistic research to social issues isn't carried out in the value-free atmosphere that is best for scientific work ... this kind of engagement [in controversies about language and thought, bilingual education, and legal language] may be far removed from the dispassionate approach to verification and disproof that's essential for good scientific work.
>
> (1982: 166)

But he concludes:

> On closer examination of the record of this research, I've come to recognise that objectivity and commitment can't be partitioned as neatly as that. Commitment is needed at all stages of this research: in entering the field; in dealing with a racist society on both sides of the issue; withstanding the kinds of criticism that I have cited above.
>
> (1982: 195)

The difficulty is that this change of view is presented as the product of experience. Although the paper offers important personal and professional testimony, its theoretical engagement with the nature of both objectivity and commitment is insufficient. It announces a dilemma but gives students and researchers inadequate guidance about the ways in which they might resolve it.

This problem was, I think, registered in the first stages of my own work. åriginally inspired by Labov, my initial plan had been to produce

51

objective evidence on linguistic structure which would contradict widespread prejudice about the English of Asian Britons. But once I realised that a new vernacular would need a community to speak it and that there were already enough stereotypes in circulation, it was no longer possible to retain confidence in this kind of advocacy. My project didn't grind to a halt: concern about stereotyping could be accommodated within more recent strands of variationist sociolinguistics, which allowed for the flexibility and multiplicity of group affiliation (Milroy 1980). In this way, it was possible to stick to an academic schedule which led to the correlation of pronunciation with social variables. But it now seemed wiser to avoid any direct political or educational implications. The way in which variationists prioritised the division between researcher and researched offered little scope for the development of a project that was sensitive to local sociolinguistic priorities, and since there are good grounds for being very cautious about practical recommendations that emanate from sources remote from the people they target, it seemed sensible not to try to make any.

Of course, ultimately, the project broke out of these constraints, but it was the ethnography of communication, not variationist sociolinguistics, that provided a satisfactory rationale for linking academic and educational concerns.

Within the ethnography of communication (EC), there are a number of well documented instances of sociolinguistic researchers carrying out projects which have succeeded in making major contributions to academic knowledge at the same time as involving local informants as active partners. The research has both drawn on local knowledge and contributed sociolinguistic perspectives which have assisted informants in the conduct of their daily lives. Shirley Brice Heath's work in the Piedmont Carolinas introduced the methods and understandings of research into local schools, and Gumperz, Jupp, Roberts and their associates linked the study of situated interaction with systematic programmes designed to raise social and communicative awareness in multiracial workplaces in Britain (Furnborough *et al.* 1982; Gumperz, Jupp and Roberts 1979; Heath 1983; for an important programmatic statement on some of the possibilities, see Hymes 1980 on ethnographic monitoring).

Of course, as with any attempt to describe a paradigm (including variationist sociolinguistics), a general account of EC runs the risk of representing it as a more unified and coherent tradition than it actually is. EC can vary from comprehensive descriptions of the place that certain speech activities have in the social life of particular communities, to fine-grained analyses of interaction in particular situations (where the term Interactional Sociolinguistics is now more commonly used). There is a danger of assuming that ethnography is inevitably radical,[11] and more widely, there is a good deal of uncertainty about ethnographer–informant relations, so that there seems to be no easily reported consensus (cf. Clifford and Marcus 1985; Geertz 1988; Strathern 1985). Nevertheless, certain characteristics can be identified which permit a more productive relationship between the researcher and researched than one finds in variationist sociolinguistics, as well as more substantial social interventions.

In the first place, accurate description of local perceptions is a basic requirement for validity in ethnography, and this means that local attitudes to language are attended to more sympathetically and represented more extensively in their own terms. Ethnography is more open-ended in its fieldwork procedures and there is less pressure to fit data into schemes that have been planned in advance (Hymes 1980). In this it contrasts with the standardised concepts and methods used in variationist investigations of attitude (cf. Labov 1981: 21–23 on subjective reaction, self-report and linguistic insecurity tests).

Variationist research generally sees its objectives as linguistic, not sociological (Labov 1972: 184; Trudgill 1978: ch. 1; Walters 1988: 126), and this inhibits examination of the cultural contexts which animate attitudes to language. In contrast, EC makes much less of this separation of language and context, and gives as much attention to order in society as organisation in language (Hymes 1974, 1980).[12] This has produced a very different contribution to the debate about linguistic equality. Whereas variationists made great public play of one insight central to the study of linguistic structure (Lyons 1968: 44–45), the ethnographer's wider concern with the relationship between language and sociocultural setting has produced a far more judicious assessment of the links between language and disadvantage, so that, for example Bernstein's theories of restricted and elaborated code have been treated much more sympathetically (compare Labov 1969 and Hymes 1973, 1980).[13] Indeed, since it served as a crucial spur to the very idea of communicative competence (Hymes 1972a), one can say that the question of linguistic disadvantage has in fact been a central inspiration in the development of the ethnography of communication as a programme of research (see again note 12).

Variationist research takes its initial cue from linguistic questions about structure, variation, change and dialect, and it is to these that it primarily addresses its reports. The agenda sketched out by Hymes (1972b) is looser: as a group, studies in the ethnography of communication cover a much wider range of language practices and often follow traditions in anthropology, where there is a recognised place for primarily descriptive accounts in which theory is implicit or largely unorganised (Hammersley and Atkinson 1983: 176; Hymes 1980: 96), and where there is a common view that theory should stay fairly close to

53

the ground (Geertz 1973: 20, 24; Hammersley and Atkinson 1983: 183). This failure to give consistent emphasis to academic theory is one frequent source of criticism (e.g. Fasold 1990: 60–62), but it does provide EC with more scope for engagement with the linguistic issues and activities that preoccupy the communities being researched.

Finally, it is worth considering certain notions of objectivity in ethnography, which can facilitate an open relationship between researcher and researched as well as clarifying the connections between research and commitment. Rather than trying to extract the researcher from the data and analysis, increasingly there is an emphasis on making the researcher's influence as explicit and accountable as possible. Objectivity depends on the investigator being visible to the reader, so that interpretation of the research can proceed with some idea of the researcher's activities and assumptions, and the relation of these to the informants' (Erikson 1977; Hymes 1980). This view provides a route through Labov's unresolved opposition between objectivity and social values. Certainly, the dispassionate execution of certain core analytical and logical procedures remains an essential, indeed constitutive, feature of investigation, but researchers need not feel that their work is invalidated if their social commitments influence their selections of topic, their methodologies, their field relationships, etc. What matters is that these influences should be accounted for as fully as possible.

This difference between variationist and ethnographic notions of objectivity allows alternative conceptions of community. Attention to cross-cultural contact in the form of the researcher–researched relationship can easily shift over from being the methodological requirement for objectivity, to being a major analytic activity in its own right. The understandings built between investigators and informants in the field may raise some informal uncertainties about the nature of group belonging: when cross-cultural communication itself becomes the theme, notions of group membership and community can no longer be accepted as fixed characteristics and well-defined totalities (cf. Gumperz 1982: 26–29). In addition, the reflexivity required by this view of objectivity can lead beyond an examination of face-to-face relations into a broader consideration of the sociopolitical links between researcher and researched, and of the parts they play in the larger contexts which embrace the identities of both.

Recognition of structural ties between the researcher and researched encourages scrutiny of the view that useful critical discussion is only possible within the academic community (if indeed that itself can be properly identified), and a number of the features described above enhance this. Certainly, theory development and hypothesis testing in ethnography require a thorough grasp of relevant research literatures, and researchers are likely to be distinguished from locals by their familiarity with a cumulative and comparative knowledge base (Hymes 1980: 73, 96, 105). Nevertheless, it has been argued that ethnographic modes of analysis are little more than systematic and clerical common sense (ibid.: 105; Heath 1983: 339, 354) and as such they are likely to be intrinsically accessible.

Of course within any project, a host of dilemmas and difficulties remain in the relationship between researcher and researched (cf. e.g. Dingwall 1980; Milroy 1987: 92; Saville-Troike 1982: 121, 1983) and, arguably, ethnographers of communication are likely to be less sanguine about the prospects of intervention and social change than others, since language use is seen as embedded within a complex sociocultural ecosystem (e.g. Erickson and Shultz 1981: 193; Heath 1983: 344, 366). But in principle, sustained involvement in particular situations permits a better view of local priorities, formulations and social divisions, facilitating forms of intervention unanticipated from outside (cf. e.g. Brooks and Roberts 1985; Cazden 1981). Overall, there seems to be some substance in Hymes's view that:

> of all forms of scientific knowledge, ethnography is the most open, the most compatible with a democratic way of life, the least likely to produce a world in which experts control knowledge at the expense of those who are studied.
>
> (1980: 105)

Those, then, are some differences in the potential for the relationship between researcher and researched offered by variationist sociolinguistics and the ethnography of communication. Broadly speaking, EC offers better scope both for dialogue and for social intervention, and this is, I think, reflected in the way that the third phase of my own research developed. During this stage, rather than directly censuring negative local attitudes to learners of ESL, I followed up the impersonations and attitudes that emerged once data collection began. Instead of hiding them, I also acknowledged aspects of my social background which had originally generated the research interest (for example, my job as an ESL teacher). And in the end, informants seemed to find this part of my research more interesting than the variationist section. The final account started to sketch out the overarching relations of knowledge, power and interdependence that link researchers and researched together, and it could be said to mediate between local and educational discourses, two groups of responses to non-proficiency in English which had developed in contiguous domains, unknown to one another despite their shared historical origins. With each of these features, it is possible to make a systematic link back to the ethnography of communication.

To end, I would like to make a resumé of the ways in which my own research, together with these two disciplinary affiliations, links into the theme of our book.

ETHICS, ADVOCACY OR EMPOWERMENT?

We have found it useful to distinguish three types of researcher–researched relationship:

(i) research on informants
(ii) research on and for informants, and
(iii) research on, for and with informants.

Each of these involves the investigator in a different type of respect for their subjects' interests and well-being.

(i) In research on, the well-being of subjects may act as a negative force, constraining what researchers would ideally like to do. We have called this kind of fairly minimalist concern for the researched 'ethical'.
(ii) In research on and for informants, efforts are made to turn the researcher's independent academic concerns to the local community's benefit. We have designated this an advocacy position.
(iii) Research on, for and with involves a recognition of intellectual compatibility between researcher and researched and this means that subjects become actively involved in the formulation and discussion of the research problem (Cain 1986: 262). This involves more than the researcher entering into dialogue in order to find out local points of view - it entails informants taking part in the construction of theories about their own experience. Although 'empowerment' is a word that needs to be used cautiously in the wider political context (where we need to reckon with a range of dimensions of power, achieved as opposed to intended advantage, and a number of other issues), within the confines of the research process, the element of *with* can be called empowering, because it places informants in the driving seat, with the aid of researchers reflexively constituting themselves as objects in a theory which they are partly shaping themselves.

There are three questions: first, where do variationist and ethnographic sociolinguistics stand in this scheme? Second, where does my own research stand? And third, what does this indicate about our three-fold classification?

With regard to the first question, it is not possible to make a simple equation between on the one hand, variationist research and advocacy, and on the other, empowerment and the ethnography of communication. Certainly, the public interventions of variationists do fall within the category of research on and for, and Labov is a very clear example. But so too could work within the ethnography of communication. Indeed, an idea of objectivity which made less of the distinction between academic (rational) and popular (irrational) knowledge would encourage more open dialogue between researchers and researched, and conceivably, this might mean that the public interventions of ethnographers were more effective.

Conversely, ethnographic belief in the rationality of local views isn't automatically empowering, inviting informants to theorise alongside the investigator. Researchers may enter into the logic of their informants without letting them into the logic of the research, and dialogue can focus exclusively on the local preoccupations and priorities, not academic ones.

Nevertheless, though they are not sufficient conditions, dialogue and a belief in local rationality are necessary conditions for drawing informants into shared control of the investigative process, and unlike the characteristics of variationist activity, they do permit a shift over from advocacy to empowerment during the research, with researchers floating ideas in a way that lets informants enter and take hold of their hypotheses and theories. The ethnography of communication has more potential as an empowering research method, and Hymes's account of *co-operative* ethnographic monitoring (1980) outlines as a programme for realising this.

What of the second question? How does my project stand within this scheme? In my own work, researcher–researched relationships were something of a mixture, with elements that, up to a point, could be linked with each of the categories (i) to (iii). Seen close up, this is probably true of a great many research studies, and it may be a necessary warning against any expectation that actual projects will be either entirely ethical, entirely advocate or entirely empowering.

Although it wasn't involved in organised campaigning, the research could be said to contain an advocate component, in so far as it was critical of some dominant orthodoxies about the language of subordinate social groups and expressed this in educational arenas. There was an effort to 'contribute to an "adequate definition of reality" upon which public opinion and public policy may be based' (AAA 1971: para. 2d), and this included the argument that in certain respects, working-class adolescent perspectives had a clearer view of historical relationships than academics and education professionals.

The feedback exercise was partly 'ethical', seeking informed consent and some guidance on publication. It also showed informants around the research's analytic heartlands, and in doing so, this dialogical element might be called at least potentially empowering. One can also add that in using interactive data collection procedures, the research inevitably gave some space to the agendas of informants, and in this sense also, it had empowering potential.

Even so, the research's limitations as an exercise in empowerment can't be ignored. It wasn't the informants who decided on what should be analysed how, and by comparison with Cameron's case study in chapter 5, informants were given relatively little control over the way in which the research finally represented them. From a large database covering a wide range of topics, informants had been given no forewarning of the particular issues that I would eventually write up. And no efforts were made to find out if the presentation of findings stimulated interests which informants might want to take up and develop in ways that might have little direct relevance to the researcher (contrast Frazer's work on photo-stories – see pp. 101–5). In fact sometimes new knowledge can be disabling, and so projects that are fully committed to empowering their informants are likely to pay much closer attention to the unpredictable consequences of emergent understanding than mine did.

So the research outlined in this chapter can only make rather muted claims to be empowering in the primarily methodological sense outlined above. The question then arises: does this matter, and are there types of empowerment that lie beyond this definition?

In the introductory chapter, we adopted a 'realist' rather than a 'relativist' position, in which we stated our belief in a social reality above and beyond the understanding of individual actors. It follows from this that the perception of informants need not be the end point of social analysis, and that empowerment can be considered beyond the context of the interpersonal relationship between researcher and researched. We made the point that empowerment defined within the boundaries of the research process need not lead to emancipation in a wider socio-political context. In certain circumstances statistical 'research-on' may be the most effective strategy in stimulating social change, and in others, research which informants themselves controlled might simply help to condemn them in their own words, producing larger social effects that worked to their disadvantage. We also noted that empowering research methods are much more likely to be used with people who are already in a position to influence supra-cognitive reality, and that the groups being researched don't automatically deserve more. In fact it is not hard to imagine situations in which researchers felt that in the interests of broader political justice, they should employ disempowering methods, which were either subversive (on-and-against) or re-educative (on-against-and-with).

So any evaluation of empowering research methodology must try to incorporate a view of social realities beyond the immediate grasp of informants. Interaction between researcher and researched is not sufficient to achieve this, and it would be on these grounds that I would justify the path eventually taken in my own project. Certainly, my informants belonged to social groups which society discriminates against, and a great deal of benefit could have accrued from a more extensive sharing of control over the research. On the other hand, the research also tried to point to large-scale connections between language, hierarchy and education. It started to identify some overarching traditions of dominance that pathologise particular groups and constitute them as objects worthy of research investigation in the first place, and it began to foreground comparatively subjugated local perspectives in a way that relativised the prevailing orthodoxy. This description of positions within and around an educational 'regime of truth' would not have been possible without a substantial period of solitary analysis, and this illustrates the complexity of the link between empowerment defined in terms of the interactive informant–investigator relationship, and empowerment defined in terms of a larger social reality. While one might often be doubtful about methodologically non-interactive research which set out to question the unjust effects of macro-social processes, a maximally interactive approach does not necessarily generate more penetrating social critique. While methodology plays an important part, it cannot serve as the only reference point in a consideration of the empowering value of a piece of research.

NOTES

I am grateful to the Economic and Social Research Council for providing me with a research studentship to carry out some of the work described in this chapter.

1 In fact the education authority where I was working closed these units a few years later. But even in the late 1980s, there still appeared to be a view that reading difficulties among children of Asian extraction could be best handled through help with ESL (DES 1988: 8).
2 At an academic level, these educational views were supported by theories about 'semilingualism'. For full discussion, see Rampton 1983, 1988 and forthcoming.
3 A lot of racism was directed at people of Bangladeshi extraction.
4 The Labovian influence in sociolinguistics is not confined to quantitative issues (language change, dialectology), but extends into discourse analysis and the ethnography of communication. His considerable influence is however perhaps most distinctive in the study of grammatical and phonological variation, and it has been in connection with this aspect of his work that Labov has made his most systematic statement about the political aspects of the relationship of researcher and researched (Labov 1982).
5 This is no longer true of all variationist research, particularly where speech accommodation theory has been influential (see e.g. Bell 1984; Trudgill 1986).
6 This is a position that perhaps finds support in speech accommodation theory (Coupland et al. 1988; Giles 1971).

7 It is worth just underlining the logical inconsistency in moving from (a) the view that languages have to be judged in their own terms to (b) a view that all languages are equal (this is clearly pointed out by Milroy and Milroy 1985: 15). (a) insists that languages can't be compared, and it can be used as an argument to contradict the idea that some languages are broken ('you can't say it's defective because you're judging it by the wrong criteria'). But if you in fact argue for (b), you are implicitly accepting the idea that languages *can* be compared.

8 For example:

> Most listeners know of linguistic varieties that they do not like, but we recognise that these feelings are very subjective and have no basis in objective linguistic fact. In particular, feelings of this sort should not be allowed to influence teachers' attitudes and policies towards children's language.
>
> (Trudgill and Giles 1978: 224)

> Judgments about 'good' and 'bad' language are, from a linguistic point of view, completely arbitrary, and without foundation.
>
> (Trudgill 1975: 35)

9 The idea that (white) linguists are in some sense artificially constructing a black ethnolinguistic identity is mentioned but not addressed (Labov 1982: 178).

10 'The results of research over 15 years have been written into the law' (Labov 1982: 194) and 'members of an oppressed people have entered an academic field, taken up the tools of linguistic research, and used them for the advancement of their nation' (ibid.: 195).

11 In so far as it entails scepticism of standardised and prescriptive social scientific methodologies and treats official versions of the social world as only one among a range of possible formulations, ethnography does bear some inclination towards subversion of establishment orders (Dingwall 1980: 873). But there is no guarantee that its methods respect the ethical norms of informants or that its findings will be used to their advantage (Dingwall 1980; Hymes 1980: 99; Saville-Troike 1982: 112).

12 In a paper addressing the relationship between linguistics and its uses, Hymes remarks:

> It is striking that we have no general perspective on language as a human problem, not even an integrated body of works in search of one. Salient problems, such as translation, multilingualism, literacy and language development, have long attracted attention, but mostly as practical matters constituting 'applications' of linguistics, rather than as proper, theoretically pertinent parts of it.
>
> (1980: 20)

He goes on to say:

> it is unusual today to think of language as something to be overcome, yet four broad dimensions of language can usefully be considered in just that way: diversity of language, medium of language (spoken, written), structure of language, and functioning of language. Of each we can ask, 1) when, where, and how it came to be seen as a problem; 2) from what vantage point it is seen as a problem (in relation to other vantage points from which it may not be so seen); 3) in what ways the problem has been

approached or overcome as a practical task and also as an intellectual, conceptual task; 4) what its consequences for the study of language itself have been; 5) what kinds of study, to which linguists might contribute, are now needed.

(1980: 21)

These passages reveal a number of central differences compared to the Labovian model of socially responsible linguistics. Whereas in Labov's account, linguistic research is primary and social action comes second, in the sketch here there is an effort to achieve a broad social understanding prior to linguistic intervention. Citizenship is antecedent to linguistics rather than vice versa. Historical and political awareness of problems precedes their linguistic scrutiny (1, 2, 5); practical approaches have as important a role in the definition of problems as purely scholastic ones (3); and linguistics cannot assume that it is a neutral tool (4). Elsewhere Hymes illustrates this last point by referring to the role of language study in imperial domination (1980: 55; see also Said 1978; Voloshinov 1973: 75; Williams 1977), and there is an element of reflexivity here missing from Labov's account. For Labov, it is the racial difference between researcher and researched that generates the social dilemmas: once this is resolved by the entry of black linguists, research can continue. For Hymes, knowledge itself can be a form of domination, and much more needs to be questioned than the researcher's ethnic background.

13 See Heath 1983 for an ethnographic study which offers some support for many of Bernstein's central concepts, even though in comparison, the ways in which Bernstein relates his ideas to empirical social reality seem rather schematic.

APPENDIX

An alternative summary of Part B of the visual display of Rampton's 1987 research findings

(some of which has now been modified or revised, partly as a result of feedback discussions)

During my study, I became very interested in how people used other people's languages in friendship groups: how kids from Afro-Caribbean and English backgrounds were using Panjabi, and how Indian, Pakistani and English kids were using West Indian patois. Another thing I noticed was how kids who spoke excellent English sometimes pretended that they didn't know much English and put on very strong Indian accents. I didn't have time to look at all of these, and in the end I only looked at the last one in detail: people pretending they didn't know much English, or putting a strong Indian accent into their English. This seems to me to raise quite a lot of complex questions, and it needs to be looked at from several sides. For example, I think that when comedians like Jim Davidson or Peter Sellers come on the television and do impersonations of Indians, this is a kind of racism. But when Indian, Pakistani, English or West Indian kids put on this broken English act with their friends, it causes laughs, usually no harm is meant and no offence is taken. So in one setting (on TV) it may be racist, but in the other (among friends) it isn't. In a way, the friendship groups may be going against the TV racism by turning it upside down. This is complicated and it is worth taking each part separately. (a) Why do I think that the TV impersonations are racist? and (b) how is it that kids are often turning this racism on its head?

Let me start with (a). First of all, remarks about Indians and Pakistanis not speaking English well, and about them saying things like 'very good, very good', go back a long way to the days of the British Empire. In 1837, the British decided to teach English in India so that they could have a class of clerks who could help them keep British rule going. At about that time British people started to use the term 'babu' in an offensive way, to describe the English that Indian people spoke. They also called English-speaking Indians 'babus', and they usually regarded them as 'half-educated', polite, passive and foolish clowns.

That started well over 100 years ago, but I think it continues today in the stereotypes of Asian people in the press and on TV. I also think it goes further than that and that this derogatory stereotype has an effect outside newspapers and entertainment. Some white people (*certainly not all*) are influenced by this stereotype so that they think that if a person is Asian, they can't speak English properly. In this way, 'not speaking English well enough' has sometimes been used as an excuse for discrimination against people from Asian backgrounds (in jobs and training opportunities). *I really do not know what happens in local schools* and many teachers may be much too sensible to believe it. But a lot of the 'experts' in colleges and universities who write about education also seem to have been influenced by the 'babu' image from the days of the British Empire. A lot of books about education say how Asian kids are only 'superficially' or 'deceptively' fluent in English, and not really normal. I have looked very carefully at what they have said, and their reasoning is weak. Also they are very culturally biased. They seem to say that kids from Asian homes will never speak English properly until they give up their parents' culture completely. Of course what they say is nonsense.

In fact nowadays, this 'babu' picture is running into quite a lot of trouble, and a number of people are saying how wrong it is. Newspapers like *The Times* try to keep it going, but Ray Honeyford lost his job partly because he used it in his writing. So those are some of the reasons why I think it's racist when comedians do Indian and Pakistani impersonations on TV. These impersonations come from the days when Britain exploited India, and they can be tied up with discrimination in Britain today. But what about (b)? What about when kids do impersonations? What about when Pakistani, West Indian, English and Indian kids put on strong Panjabi accents or pretend that they can't speak much English? Why isn't that racist in the same way?

First of all, it isn't racist because talking and joking with friends who are your equals and who you know and like, is very different from talking to strangers, or to people who you don't know very well or who you aren't on equal terms with. You can say things to friends and they can say things to you which would be offensive if you didn't trust each other and if you didn't think you had a lot in common.

Second, it isn't racist because it often turns the 'babu' idea upside down. Sometimes Asian kids may put on an Indian accent and pretend that they don't understand what is happening, or act as though they think everything is very good: they may pretend that they're not in control. In fact they are taking an idea which says Asian people are powerless and turning it inside out: they are putting on this act and using it as a kind of power for themselves. For example, I've heard stories about Asian kids doing this so that they don't have to do what a teacher tells them; or sometimes they do it to tease someone. This act is used in other ways as well. In general, I think it is a way of recognising the prejudice in a lot of British society: at the same time it turns it into a source of humour which can unite kids from different ethnic back-grounds. West Indian and English kids sometimes put on this act too, though I think it may be more difficult for them than for Asian kids because there's more of a risk that people will think that they're being racist. My guess is that they need to be with good friends before they do it: there's also no doubt that when *some* kids put on this act, they *are* being racist.

There is also a third reason why it isn't racist when Asian kids and their friends put a very Panjabi accent into their English. Sometimes the 'babu' stereotype from the TV and from the days of the British Empire has got nothing to do with it at all. Sometimes, kids may be putting on an act but the people they are copying have got nothing to do with racism. For example, if an Asian kid is playing cricket and he puts on an Indian accent, maybe he's pretending to be like a World Cup cricketer. Sometimes, if they're talking to older people who don't know much English, kids may use a Panjabi accent to make it easier for the older people to understand. And perhaps sometimes they may feel like saying something in Panjabi but because the person they're talking to doesn't speak it they have to use English words although they can keep the Panjabi accent (this may work the other way round too, with kids who can only speak English wanting to use Panjabi).

So those are some of the ways in which it isn't racist when kids who speak excellent English put on a Panjabi accent and pretend they don't know much English. *In fact*, speaking with an accent and not knowing much English are two completely different things: lots of people with an accent use very good English, although in British society a lot of people don't recognise this (though some do).

In fact I think bilingual Indian and Pakistani kids in particular know two ways of looking at English. In India and Pakistan, English has a lot of prestige and not everybody is expected to be able to speak it: people who do speak English may have high status. At home in Britain and in the adult community, bilingual Indian and Pakistani kids know a lot of people who have the same view. In white British society however, English is the ordinary language: it doesn't have any special status and everyone is expected to know it. A lot of the time, people who *don't* know English get looked down on. At school, kids from Indian and Pakistani backgrounds can see this attitude, and they also see how people who don't know much English lose out in education: in fact *everyone* at school is pretty hard on kids who don't know much English (for example, quite a few Bangladeshi kids get a lot of trouble). But at home, Indian and Pakistani kids maybe see things differently: it doesn't matter if people talk with an accent and kids often help and support their parents if they don't know much English. Maybe they also enjoy it if parents are proud of their kids' English, and give them special responsibilities because of it. Indeed because of these things, Indian and Pakistani kids may be more confident in using English than other kids.

Perhaps putting on an act and pretending not to know much English is a way of reconciling these two views of the language.

3

BILINGUALISM IN THE PERUVIAN ANDES

Penelope Harvey

This chapter describes an anthropological research project undertaken in a bilingual community of Quechua/Spanish speakers in the Southern Peruvian Andes (Harvey 1987a).[1] My initial aim was to look at the use of bilingualism as a political resource, and at the role of language in the establishment and maintenance of hierarchical social relations. I was particularly interested to explore the relationship between power and symbolic practice, and decided to concentrate on language use as a key example of the mundane symbolic production in which power relations are constituted and challenged. As the research went on I became increasingly aware of the complexity of local understandings of power and began to look at how people conceptualised power, how they experienced its force and how they actively produced its meaning. What I had not even remotely considered at the time of writing my research proposal was the importance that drunkenness was to play in my research, both as the site of explicit discussion of social tension and also as the moment in which language was quite specifically called upon to ride out such tensions. The relationship between drunkenness, personal empowerment and language use came to form one of the primary axes of my research findings (Harvey 1987a, 1991, 1992).

I spent many weeks when I first arrived in Peru deciding where to carry out this project. Given that I wanted to study the contestation of power as well as its assertion I deliberately sought out a research site where social tensions were overt and where these tensions were themselves closely associated with particular linguistic forms. The Southern Peruvian Andes is extremely interesting in this respect. The Spanish and Quechua languages are closely and complexly linked to local experiences of Spanish colonialism and to enduring images of the hierarchical relationships between the urban centres and the rural settlements, between the ruling classes and the peasantry, between the educated and the illiterate. Furthermore this hierarchy is reproduced in increasingly compact spheres of social relations so that social positioning is highly relative and as a result overtly contested and negotiated.

I found an example of this microcosm of complex hierarchical social relations in the town of Ocongate and the adjoining community of Chakachimpa, where I began my research in 1983. Ocongate, a town with a population of about 800, is in many respects a rural settlement, whose inhabitants are aware of their subordination to the financial and political forces of the cities. Nevertheless Ocongate is also a district capital and as such the focus of local politics, of state services and of the major religious institutions active in the locality.[2] Within this small town there was thus ample opportunity for observing the everyday interaction of people of differing socio-economic, political, educational and linguistic status. The 500 or so inhabitants of Chakachimpa were relatively disadvantaged in these respects and there was a somewhat ambiguous social division between Ocongate and Chakachimpa. This in turn was echoed by the class and cultural tensions that existed in the relationship between the valley settlements (which included both Ocongate and Chakachimpa) and the smaller communities of the high *puna* lands above the village.[3]

Before looking in detail at the research methods which I used in this study I should first outline the basic theoretical orientation that influenced the kind of knowledge I was seeking to acquire. Within the body of sociological and anthropological literature I was extremely interested in Bourdieu's work on the relationship between political struggle and the appropriation of the symbolic (Bourdieu 1977; Bourdieu and Passeron 1977), but in relation to the study of language use it was the work of Bakhtin and Voloshinov that I found particularly suggestive (Bakhtin 1981, Voloshinov 1973). As early as 1929 Voloshinov had argued that meaning as system should not be distinguished from meaning in use, as the insistence on such a distinction reified and naturalised the contingent force of political control. Meanings are social and multiple. They do battle with one another and the politics of language use essentially concerns a struggle for the imposition of meaning. This approach seemed to suggest that meanings are always and everywhere constituted in historically and culturally specific environments and that any study of the politics of language use would need to take account of both macro- and micro-historical processes as well as the details of the linguistic utterances themselves.

Work within anthropology and the sociology of language had produced important insights into the politics of language use, particularly in the areas of nationalism, language planning and ethnicity in which both macro- and micro-processes were addressed, but there was little discussion of language use on an interpersonal level, and thus no real account of the linguistic construction of meaning (e.g. Cole and Wolf 1974; Fishman 1968, 1971–2, 1974, 1978). Even studies in the ethnography of speaking rarely used tape-recordings of speech (Bauman and Sherzer

1974; Bloch 1975; Hymes 1974). Furthermore there was a tendency to concentrate on speech events that were marked in contrast to everyday linguistic interactions, often as part of ritual (see Bloch 1976).

I thus looked to sociolinguistics and discourse analysis for models of how to analyse everyday interpersonal linguistic interaction. The work of Gumperz was particularly useful, as his analyses of recorded speech focused on strategy, repertoire and the multiplicity of meaning and thus provided a point of contact between the broader social and theoretical concerns discussed above. Equally important was Gumperz's stress on communication as an interpretative process which involves negotiation and which can thus become the locus of political struggle (Gumperz 1982a, 1982b; Gumperz and Hymes 1972). Discourse analysis in turn demonstrated many of the complex ways in which linguistic utterances are themselves constitutive of the interactional context (Schegloff 1972; Schiffrin 1987; Van Dijk 1985). However, in themselves, these approaches appeared remarkably unconcerned with the workings of broader patterns of social reality within which human subjects act, that is with gender, class, race and generation. These were treated as givens, as constraints on interaction. My intention was thus to combine the detailed study of interaction with the more general anthropological and socio-logical understandings of social relations.

Methodologically the bringing together of these two approaches implied the combination of the long period of participant observation in the field favoured in anthropological research with the collection of tape-recorded linguistic data essential to sociolinguistic study. In sub-sequent sections of this chapter I discuss in some detail these two basic methods which I used to carry out this research. I then go on to discuss some of the implications of the ways in which I used these methods. I pay particular attention to the relationship between researcher and researched, the setting of agendas and the question of accountability and feedback. Finally I suggest that there is a sense in which principles of advocacy and empowerment can usefully be combined in research of this kind.

As students we were generally discouraged from getting involved in advocacy roles, taking up causes of the people with whom we were going to work. We were advised that such activities were likely to be personally distracting, frustrating, even dangerous and would jeopardize the com-pletion of the Ph.D. thesis within the four-year time limit set by the Economic and Social Research Council. This government funding body drew up a black list of institutions whose average completion rate across the various departments of a university was deemed unsatisfactory and cut all post-graduate social science research funding to these institutions. The measure was applied retrospectively and students were placed under strong moral pressure to complete as rapidly as possible and not to endanger future post-graduate research. Appeasing the personal conscience of historical guilt at the expense of future research was not encouraged.

Nevertheless, in pre-fieldwork seminars I discussed ethics at length with fellow students, and there was general consensus that we should do everything possible to limit damage to the researched. In retrospect I think we over-rated our power and influence. British anthropologists are no longer the representatives of a colonial power, necessarily providing information that could be used to aid Britain's policies of indirect rule and political intervention. By comparison with the influence of contemporary imperialist institutions such as the World Bank and the US State Department the presence of a few anthropologists is politically insignificant. Peruvian culture did not seem in danger of being rocked by the arrival of a British post-graduate student. Nevertheless, as I will discuss, the power of representation was mine and I was thus concerned to guard the anonymity of informants in any written documents and not to betray people's trust (having at the time no idea of what such trust might relate to or concern). I certainly aimed to be as sensitive as possible to my informants' demands and needs, yet to take a basically non-interventionist position. Politically I did not think it appropriate for me to set the agenda for empowerment of a group about whom I as yet knew nothing. While I hoped that my work might reveal something useful about the workings of power, a concept whose meaning I was far from clear about, I quite consciously did not feel that it was my place to act on such research findings. This position is obviously related to contemporary awareness within anthropology of the politics of textual representation, and the subsequent stress on the moment of such representation as the point of appropriate political intervention.

RESEARCH METHODS

Participant observation

Participant observation is the method which has traditionally distinguished anthropology from other approaches to the study of human social life. The method in itself does not imply a particular epistemology; it has been used to support positivist approaches as well as both realist and relativist positions. Indeed, many aspects of this fieldwork method have remained basically unchanged since the late nineteenth century when the earliest ethnographers began to collect systematic data for their own analyses (Stocking 1987).

Anthropological fieldwork necessarily involves intensive interaction between the researcher and the researched. The researcher should ideally live in the community, learn the local language or languages, engage in the activities of daily life, and try to understand why and how people do what they do. While the research may concern particular agendas, which reflect the intellectual preoccupations of the time, this intense involvement in the daily life of the research subjects has meant that information is always gathered on many aspects that are not of immediate or obvious relevance. Indeed, any aspect of the seemingly strange and opaque behaviours of the subject community may inform the researcher's understanding of their particular research topic.

Participation is thus essential to the anthropological method, as is the ignorance and alienation experienced by the anthropologist in the subject community. As Lévi-Strauss has commented:

> Research in the field, by which every anthropological career begins, is mother and nurse of doubt. ... This 'anthropological doubt' does not only consist of knowing that one knows nothing, but of resolutely exposing what one thought one knew – and one's very ignorance – to buffetings and denials directed at one's most cherished ideas and habits by other ideas and habits best able to rebut them.
>
> (Lévi-Strauss 1978: 26)

This intensely subjective experience of alienation and feelings of social inadequacy, referred to by Wagner as 'culture shock', leads the researcher first to objectify the other culture as part of the process of 'learning' its ways, and then in turn to objectify her own culture as a concrete instance of difference in terms of which the researched are contrasted, articulated and ultimately understood (Wagner 1975). It is thus possible to see from this perspective why anthropology has tended to concentrate on the study of social groups in which the researchers themselves are not implicated. However this necessary distance between researcher and researched also implies that 'the knowledge of the object [the researched] does not reach intrinsic properties but is limited to expressing the relative and ever-shifting position of the subject [the researcher] in relation to it' (Lévi-Strauss 1978: 27).

Thus it is that the history of anthropological method has more to do with the shifting position of the researcher than the concrete practices by which the fieldwork itself is carried out. Similarly, 'experience' via participant observation, has consistently provided the basis for ethnographic authority, even in contemporary postmodern accounts where such authority is consciously exposed in the text itself as an artefact of the act of writing. In the remainder of this section I discuss four moments in the history of anthropological method in order to illustrate these continuities and to show that the changes in the discipline essentially relate to anthropologists' understandings of what they are observing and recording rather than the methods by which they observe and record. This brief account of how anthropology has constructed its research object has important bearing on the extent to which anthropological research might be empowering to research subjects.

Malinowski is often taken as the founding figure of British social anthropology and his early insistence on participant observation as the primary fieldwork method has been highly influential.[4] Malinowski's understanding of society and culture was of an integrated social reality. He believed that particular behaviours should be understood in terms of how they functioned as part of this wider whole. Researchers were thus observing facts about society, social facts that held meaning in terms of the wider context of which they were a part. Taken together these observed facts could be used to formulate hypotheses about general laws of nature and society which could in theory be submitted to scientific experiment and control. Anthropology was thus perceived in this approach as an inductive and empirical science.

Malinowski placed great importance on the act of writing as a central feature of his systematic fieldwork method. Writing converts the raw experience of the ethnographer into data, and the distinctions which Malinowski and his followers made concerning types of data reveal the ways in which this initial classification of subjective experience itself creates and objectifies the categories from which the ethnography, the product of the research process, is later constructed. Malinowski basically distinguished three kinds of data. The first of these concerned the statements and observations required to build up the sets of rules and customs which organise the daily lives of the research subjects. He would chart which customs were related to particular activities, the elements of particular activities and the connections between such elements. His method was one of 'statistic documentation by concrete evidence' and the object was to 'provide the empirical investigator with a mental chart, in accordance with which he can take his bearings and lay his course' (Malinowski 1922: 12–13). The second kind of data related to what Malinowski termed 'the imponderabilia of everyday life', the mundane events and behaviours that work both with and against the general rules. This detail was recorded on a daily basis in the ethnographic diary. Third there were the 'ethnographic statements, characteristic narratives, typical utterances, items of folk-lore and magical formulae', which were seen to provide a corpus of information on native mentality. Finally it is also interesting to note that Malinowski produced a fourth kind of documentation, his personal diaries (Malinowski 1967), which, given his concern to convince his readers that 'the facts he was putting before them were objectively acquired, not subjective creations' (Clifford 1988: 29), were perceived by him at the time to provide a 'safety valve, a means of channelling the personal cares and emotions of the ethnographer away from his scientific notes' (Kuper 1977: 27).

The final stage of anthropological research requires the researcher to use the data collected in the field to write the ethnography. In Malinowski's case the ethnography was to be an integrated explanation of the functioning of social life describing simultaneously what people say they do, what they actually do and what they think (Kuper 1977: 29–30). These positivist texts typically gave considerable space to the 'native's point of view' but the ethnographer always controlled all analysis and interpretation. The author was typically absent from the text, just as his subjective experience was abstracted into the personal diaries which were not seen as part of the scientific data which the study set out to present.

The work of Lévi-Strauss provides an interesting contrast to Malinowski and the British empiricists. Lévi-Strauss did fieldwork among the native peoples of Brazil and collected and recorded data in a similar fashion to Malinowski. He also believed in the necessity of a scientific approach to anthropological research, and in the importance of the comparative method for understanding human culture. However, Lévi-Strauss had a quite different conception of what it was that the fieldworker was observing and recording. His great contribution to anthropology was his insistence on the symbolic nature of the anthropological object – social life – and his realisation that symbolic structures could not be empirically observed. He believed that the anthropologist's task was to learn a way of thinking and to present the logic of this thought in the ethnography. The data collected in the field were needed to build up an understanding of the conceptual structures that inform the behaviour of the researched. The model Lévi-Strauss employed for tracing the relationship between the observable phenomena of daily life and the invisible organising structure was taken from linguistics, which seemed to offer an attractive formal and rigorous framework for pursuing a generalizing descriptive science. Thus Lévi-Strauss pictured social anthropology as 'a taxonomy whose purpose is to identify and to classify types, to analyse their constituent parts and to establish correlations between them' (Lévi-Strauss 1978: 12). However in contrast to the approach of Malinowski he did not view these correlations as 'external and of fact, but internal and of reason' (Lévi-Strauss 1978: 23). Thus it is that the written accounts of these two authors are so radically distinct because Lévi-Strauss aimed to explicate the workings of highly abstracted mental models while Malinowski constructed positivist descriptions of the workings of observable social phenomena.

Despite the radical differences in how society was conceptualised by functionalists and structuralists, both groups nevertheless thought of their object of study as a coherent and homogeneous whole. By the 1970s and throughout the 1980s this certainty in the coherent nature of the anthropological object began to break down. The colonized peoples

71

of the Third World were beginning to put forward versions of the nature of social life in terms of their own experience, and an emergent feminism was also indicating that the omniscient vision of the absent author masked a plurality of equally valid understandings of culture and society.

Clifford Geertz is the anthropologist most commonly associated with the emergence of this critique of ethnographic authority. He too followed the traditional fieldwork method of participant observation and ethnographic documentation, in his case on the island of Bali. Geertz adapted the social philosophies of hermeneutics and pheno-menology to anthropological fieldwork. Once again the overall purpose of anthropological research was redefined and was now presented as an act of interpretation (Geertz 1973). He stressed that anthropology is not an experimental science in search of laws, but an interpretative exercise in search of meaning. Geertz's textual authority still centres on the experiential nature of fieldwork and the notion that the participant observer can come to understand the ways in which the researched understand or interpret human behaviour with reference to the webs of meaning which constitute a culture. The task of the ethnographer is thus to elucidate the symbolic practice of a particular culture. When the anthropologist interprets an event rather than merely describes it, she is involved in 'thick description', a term Geertz borrowed from the philosopher Gilbert Ryle, who illustrates the concept by differentiating between merely noting the external appearance of an action (e.g. a rapidly contracting eyelid), and interpreting that event, engaging in 'thick description' (e.g. noting the action as winking, twitching, pretend-ing to twitch, etc.).

> Thus textualisation generates sense through a circular movement that isolates and then contextualizes a fact or event in its englobing reality. A familiar mode of authority is generated that claims to represent discrete, meaningful worlds. Ethnography is the inter-pretation of cultures.
>
> (Clifford 1988: 39)

Geertz's work opened the way for what has been termed a dialogic anthropology in which researchers consciously attempt to locate them-selves in the texts which they produce, and to reveal that the cultural representations embodied in ethnographic texts are the negotiated outcome of the interactions between researcher and researched (Agar 1986, Clifford 1988, Clifford and Marcus 1986, Rabinow and Sullivan 1979, Strathern 1985).

> It becomes necessary to conceive of ethnography not as the experience and interpretation of a circumscribed 'other' reality,

but rather as a constructive negotiation involving at least two, and usually more, conscious, politically significant subjects. Paradigms of experience and interpretation are yielding to discursive paradigms of dialogue and polyphony.

(Clifford 1988: 41)

Finally, this attention to the role of the researcher in the construction of the research data has also led to a reflexive anthropology which emphasises the inevitability of researchers constructing such dialogues in terms of their own subjective understandings of the interaction. Influences from literary criticism and the new history have focused the attention of anthropologists on the ways in which they represent their field experiences in the ethnography (Bakhtin 1981, Derrida 1976, Whyte 1978). Now it is not just 'fact', but also 'memory' and 'experience' which are open to analysis and deconstruction. In this debate the fieldnotes themselves begin to lose their central importance as the privileged stores of knowledge.

> The working out of understandings may be symbolized by field-notes, but the intellectual activities that support such understandings are unlikely to be found in the daily records. The great dependency commonly claimed to exist between fieldnotes and fieldworkers is not and cannot be so very great at all ... the heavy glop of material we refer to as fieldnotes is necessarily incomplete and insufficient. It represents the recorded memory of a study perhaps, but it is only a tiny fraction of the fieldworker's own memory of the research period. ... Impressionist tales [Van Maanen's term for this particular genre of ethnography] draw attention not only to the culture of study but also to the way a fieldworker's location and experience in the field help him to produce a text to interpret.

(Van Maanen 1988: 118)

It is interesting to note that even at this stage when the ethnography seems to have moved so far away from Malinowski's realist texts, the 'raw' fieldwork data is still basically of the same order. The difference is that the personal motivations, reactions and preoccupations which Malinowski consciously separated out as a by-product of the research process are here reproduced as the central and defining feature of the final text.

Thus we have reached a point in anthropology where the automatic authority of the fieldwork experience is somewhat displaced as writers seek to analyse the discursive tropes that they are forced to use in order to organise knowledge and its representation. While some think of this moment as the crisis of an anthropology which has failed to meet the challenge of post-colonial and feminist politics (Hart 1990), others feel that anthropology has achieved a self-consciousness that at last allows it to investigate the ways in which power shapes anthropological practice and representation.

In terms of our present concerns with notions of objectivity and observer interference, participant observation obviously complicates the idea of the detached observer. Indeed many anthropologists have felt despair at how the gruelling demands of participation in many subsistence economies leaves little energy or enthusiasm for any 'observation' at all. This research technique forces the observer to work with *people*, from whom linguistic utterances cannot be abstracted in the actual collection of the data, although abstraction obviously occurs in the process of writing, a topic to which I will return.

In the small communities in which much anthropological work takes place personal relationships are extremely intense. The emotional and physical dependence experienced by the researcher is perhaps necessarily played down in final accounts – usually left out altogether or referred to in an introductory chapter – yet such relationships make it inevitable that research agendas are constantly negotiated during the process of fieldwork itself, in the same way as the researcher/researched relationship is.

In this sense informants have considerable control over the kinds of data that a researcher can collect and the occasions on which they can be collected. The research process itself reveals the limits within which a researcher's presence as researcher is tolerated. Obviously what does and does not count as intrusive or inappropriate behaviour is very difficult to know in advance. I was worried about attending the funeral of somebody I had never met; I was concerned over the inconvenience I might be causing when I moved into a peasant household; I felt uneasy when I asked people direct questions about their sex lives and about their most intimate personal relationships. However, such concerns on my part were often not only unfounded but on occasions even ridiculed. On the other hand people felt rejected when I would not get drunk with them; they expressed disapproval of some of my personal relationships; and they could be hurt and upset by my inept handling of financial matters. There were occasions when my presence required active participation and other occasions where it was more appropriate simply to watch, either because of my lack of skill or because of some aspect of my identity – such as my gender, my age, my status as researcher or daughter – was deemed inappropriate. Overall I was lucky, people somehow expected me to be stupid and to behave inappropriately and I managed never to transgress basic morality nor to create enemies among those who had the influence to end my stay in the community. Nevertheless, I frequently experienced the rage of impotence as I felt bound to meet demands I found unreasonable and as I was forced to accept severe limitations on my personal space and autonomy.

I mention these aspects of my fieldwork experience to emphasise the fact that the relationship between researcher and researched cannot be depicted as a straightforwardly hierarchical one in which the researcher simply imposes an agenda. The interactive nature of participant observation implies considerable autonomy for the researched at the moment of data collection and their agendas necessarily become part of the overall research process. The relative weighting of distinctive agendas thus emerges as a problem and is an issue to which I return below.

It is also important to emphasise that the researcher has only limited control over which members of any given research community are actually going to participate in the research process. Unlike the other researchers in this book, I did not occupy a recognised position within the social hierarchy of the research community and my ability to research was totally dependent on the extent to which people were prepared to accept my presence as a feature of their daily lives.

The family which first welcomed me into its house was a powerful and influential one. My initial contact taught in the University of Cusco and it was he who initially suggested that I go to Ocongate. His elder brother first took me there and invited me to stay in his house. The family, A, was wealthy in local terms, its members well-educated and their political influence in the district considerable. However, I soon realised that if I were to be successful in learning Quechua, and in participating in the daily lives of people of less privileged status, then I would do better to try and live in Chakachimpa. I was therefore taken to the house of B, the woman who had raised the now parental generation of family A, and who was attached to this family by bonds of spiritual kinship or godparenthood as they had sponsored her marriage. B and her husband C initially took me in out of respect for her godparents. Towards the end of my initial two-year period of fieldwork and on a subsequent field trip I lived with their eldest son and his wife. They had a house in Ocongate and living with them allowed me a further opportunity to experience yet another facet of life in this village.

Finally I also had very close contact with the family of my research assistant, a returned migrant from the capital Lima, and now a successful trader from Chakachimpa. As a research assistant he was to an extent self-selected. I had initially thought of working with a woman but the woman in question lost interest, or perhaps never really had any, and he volunteered for the job.

I used both the Spanish and Quechua languages in my work. My own speech was predominantly in Spanish although I would address monolinguals to the best of my ability in Quechua. However, my passive understanding of the language was sufficient for me to glean considerable information from linguistic interaction in Quechua. All the Quechua material was transcribed and translated by native Quechua speakers in Peru.

I had very close and frequent contact with members of 45 of the 187 separate households of Ocongate and Chakachimpa (91 in Ocongate and 96 in Chakachimpa). I was frequently invited into these houses and would spend my days with the household members. I also had regular access to members of another 64 households. My relationship to this second group was less intimate but they were people whom I met regularly in the daily life of the village. The final group of 78 households I knew less well or not at all. Many would have been introduced to me but I never talked at length with any of them and the basic data I have on these households were given to me by other people. Finally I had some contact with households in the high *puna* area but at no time did I spend an extended period there.

I outline this detail concerning informants to emphasise that those with whom I had particularly close relationships and from whom I gathered most of my information were not simply selected by me as optimum sources of information. Although I was always conscious of trying to keep a balance of the kinds of people that I got to know well, reflected in my moving from one house to another, the people themselves were actively engaged in the relationships that developed between us. These relationships were always far more complex than the emotionally sterilized terminology of researcher/researched suggests. Members of the original family treated me as someone who, like them, could appreciate the interesting aspects of 'their indigenous culture and language', conceptual entities which they themselves maintained a certain distance from. B and C were calling me their daughter within a week of arriving at their house and I fitted into their family through this fictional but nevertheless functional positioning. In time several families invited me to baptise their children and we thus became linked by ties of godparenthood which again became an important aspect of these relationships and differentiated them from others I had in the village.

The relationship with my research assistant was perhaps the most interesting. On the one hand he treated me as his employer. I made demands of him, he complied, sometimes uneasily. Yet he was also aware that he was employed to help me to know how to behave and to make sense of what was going on around me. In this respect the relationship reversed and I sometimes had to act in ways that made me uneasy. The power dynamic in this relationship was under constant negotiation, he was my lifeline and the bane of my life, to him I was a source of both prestige and shame. His relationship to me also altered significantly depending on who else we were interacting with and how he positioned himself and me *vis-à-vis* them.

The relationship between researcher and researched is thus as much a part of the process of social interaction as are the relationships between the researched themselves. The observer is necessarily an integral factor in all observed interaction and as such a valid source of interactional data. The fact that the relationship between researcher and researched is necessarily under constant negotiation and re-evaluation also has important implications for the negotiation of research agendas. One of the advantages of this research method, as opposed to more structured interviews or questionnaires, is that the research agenda is left deliberately loose or open-ended in order to allow for the emergence of those ideas and concerns salient and relevant to the researched. Thus, in my case, I had to identify the ways in which the issue of language and power was relevant to my informants. In this sense it was vital and axiomatic that informants be treated as active subjects. Anthropology is very good at this dimension of the research relationship, there is no question of simply dismissing other people's views and opinions because they do not coincide with our own, because this lack of coincidence becomes the central point of explanation. I believe this to be a distinctive and valuable contribution of participant observation as a method, despite the fact that our own cultural lenses often prevent us from understanding or even noticing such differences and despite the tendency to homogenize and over-generalize the views and opinions of such research subjects.

Tape-recorded data

At the beginning of this chapter I stressed the importance of collecting tape-recorded data in order to understand the ways in which meanings are constituted in linguistic interactions. In my research these recorded interviews or conversations were not used to provide examples of 'natural language', nor did I conceive of such data as more objective or as less affected by the presence of the researcher than those interactions in which I did not record. Indeed, once faced with the complexity of human social interaction, lingering Labovian concerns with observer-affected interviews and consciously controlled linguistic production – not to mention the notions of unified subject and continuous traditions that underlie the concepts of speaker, domain and event – actually impeded rather than aided my research. My initial attempts to abstract a social context to which particular linguistic forms could be related were constantly frustrated, even in the apparently simple task of deciding who the interlocutors were. Among my informants class was talked about and conceived in terms of race, racial categories were highly relative and hard to pin down, age was a continuum with no stable meaningful divisions, and gender derived its meaning from a complex set of masculinities and femininities closely related but never equivalent to the status markers of class, race and age. The social value of such categories as did emerge was negotiated in the interaction itself, and it was thus impossible to work within a framework that assumed fixed identities (such as Black working-class male) and unambiguous power relations.

My recordings were nevertheless obtained in two ways, in formal tape-recorded interviews, and in conversations recorded without the informants' knowledge. I will discuss these in turn.

The formal interviews were those occasions when I specifically went to ask for answers to particular questions and tape-recorded the answers with the informants' knowledge. In these interviews I would ask people to tell me their life histories, I would discuss beliefs in, for example, the supernatural, or ask for explanations of particular social behaviours, such as kinship and godparenthood. Formal interviews are obviously quite different from participant observation. People can and do refuse to answer questions but once they engage in the process the researcher tends to occupy the technologically superior position (recording and writing) and also occupies a socially marked space – associated with the prestige of education and the institutionalised power of government officials such as census takers.

Interviews as a research technique have been widely discussed (Briggs 1986). People tell you what they think you want to hear and certainly do not tell you what they do not want you to know. I found such interviews most useful in terms of identifying acceptable ways in which people could discuss certain topics with me. I also used the technique to try and speed up the process of participant observation – to get ideas about aspects of people's lives that might not have occurred to me. On the whole these interviews were taped more with a view to content analysis than to the analysis of linguistic form, although the two did overlap to some degree, especially in terms of moves between Quechua and Spanish in reported speech and the lexical items and metaphors that people used to explain things to me. Although the formal interview is more restricted than participant observation in terms of negotiating research agendas, that negotiation will still be going on in the process of interpretation as speaker and hearer work towards their respective interactive goals, drawing on assumptions and knowledges that do not necessarily coincide. Briggs (1986) has shown that sensitive use of interview material could be used by researchers to identify conflicting understandings of research objectives, which presumably could in turn be used as a starting point from which to make distinctive or conflicting agendas explicit.

Covert recording

On other occasions I would tape conversations covertly, hiding a Walkman-sized recorder in a pocket or bag. This technique was employed particularly to obtain examples of drunken conversations and arguments. Clandestine taping is of course very contentious methodologically, and a practice which we question in the opening chapter of this book. It is definitely a practice which makes me feel uncomfortable and which I can quite easily construct as a betrayal of trust on my part. However, after much consideration I realise that I cannot simply dismiss the use of this technique as an error of uninformed youth! Given the nature of the project I do not think that I would necessarily act differently on another occasion. It is thus the nature of the research project which I felt necessitated this methodology, that is, the investigation of the ways in which langauge is constitutive of hierarchical social relations.

Recordings of drunken speech were central to this enterprise. People who were normally quiet and seemingly submissive in public would talk a lot when drunk, would shout, sing, laugh and cry with no preoccupation for the effect their words would have on others or the disapproval that they might provoke. There were also important links between drinking and the supernatural world as, on the whole, drinking sessions involved communication with the major spirit powers of the area, not to mention the fact that most drinking sessions took place during religious festivals. The most salient feature of drunken speech is the release it affords from constraints of sober interaction – constraints which centre on general interactional norms of showing respect, practising avoidance rather than confrontation, being very shy and quiet in a public gathering and avoiding any show of emotion. These constraints tie into Bourdieu's concept of practical competence – by which he refers to the competence not only to speak but also to make oneself heard (Bourdieu and Passeron 1977). Practical competence is the ability to embed utterances in strategies which are tacitly adjusted to the relations of force between speakers. The idea is that if people lack the symbolic 'capital' to endow their speech with authority and thus be heard, then they will remain silent. The use of Quechua and Spanish was particularly interesting in this respect as people who would not normally use Spanish would use it profusely when drunk. Drinking alcohol results in altered states of consciousness. The perception of the constraints of the social system are altered and with it people's assessment of their own practical competence. As a result the implicit social knowledge explored in ritual, the recognition of the contradictions inherent in power relations, is made explicit in drunken speech. People would swing from joyful assertion of their strength and ability for hard work to a despairing recognition of their poverty. They would take pride in their Inka ancestry yet weep that their Indianness constituted their powerlessness. They would bemoan their loneliness in the midst of communal celebrations, and they would voice grievances and resentments that were never articulated publicly when sober.

Having realised the importance of such speech to my overall project I felt it necessary to obtain tape-recordings that would be analysed not simply on the level of lexicon and the choice of Spanish or Quechua but also for the occurrence of features such as stress, pitch, speed, intonation, the use of pauses and the turn-taking procedures through which people negotiated their positions in the interaction. With respect to the effect of my presence, the data obtained in this way were qualitatively different from the data obtained in formal interviews. Although my presence was always part of the interaction, conversations where the tape-recorder was not obviously present did not focus on me in the same way. My agendas were therefore both less explicit and also less constraining. Furthermore my concern was not that particular linguistic features would be consciously monitored by informants were they to become conscious of the tape-recorder, but rather that the discussion of particular topics and particular kinds of interaction might not occur at all. Even if drunks had spoken freely themselves they would probably have been silenced by more sober friends and relations. Indeed this did happen to me when I openly taped an interview with a man who was getting progressively drunker as the evening wore on. His wife kept trying to get him to stop talking as she was worried that he might regret having said certain things.

I was thus concerned that people might be inhibited by the fact that I was taping, because culturally drunken speech and behaviour is 'forgotten' after the event. I was aware of the fact that my own cultural norms made me embarrassed about overtly recording such conversations. Codes of acceptable practice in our culture distinguish the experience of an event, i.e. being party to a conversation, from the representation of that event. The problem was not that I overheard or listened to the conversations but that to tape a conversation is somehow to put it 'on the record' and thus to change its status.

Obviously, the fact that I controlled whether statements were on or off the record in this way, through my possession of the technology and my access to a readership to whom I could publish what I found out, emphasises the unequal relationship between me and the people of Ocongate. That such a power relationship should exist is itself problematic for anthropology and a topic for much discussion and re-examination within the profession.

It remains the case that the ethnographer's translation/representation of a particular culture is inevitably a textual construct, that as representation it cannot normally be contested by the people to whom it is attributed, and that as a 'scientific text' it eventually becomes a privileged element in the potential stores of historical memory for the nonliterate society concerned, in modern and modernizing societies, inscribed records have a greater power to shape, to reform, selves and institutions than folk memories do. They even construct folk memories. The anthropologist's monograph may return, retranslated, into a 'weaker' Third World language. In the long run, therefore, it is not the personal authority of the ethnographer, but the social authority of his ethnography that matters. And that authority is inscribed in the institutionalized forces of industrial capitalist society which are constantly tending to push the meanings of various Third World societies in a single direction. This is not to say that there are no resistances to this tendency. But 'resistance' in itself indicates the presence of a dominant force.

(Asad 1986: 163)

My concern here is to discuss whether clandestine taping necessarily and always constitutes an abuse of that power. Culturally drunken speech should be off the record. At the same time involvement in drinking sessions is a necessary aspect of participation, perhaps the most important demonstration of trust and good will and certainly an explicitly requested behaviour. These two requirements are, however, highly conflictive. The information imparted in these sessions is extremely powerful and emotive and thus necessarily influences any future interpretation of social practices. Nor does this problem end with drunken speech. Once an anthropologist begins to write, not only material such as my examples of drunken speech but also the casual conversations, comments and practices of everyday life are put on the record, whether or not a tape-recorder has been used. In this sense, although I would agree that the method is problematic, it is important to recognise that the problem arises from the relationship between representation and authorship in anthropology as a whole rather than because of the fact that the tape-recorder is hidden. In other words, it is the relationship between researcher as member of a particular and powerful social group and that of the researched as members of less powerful groups that constitutes *all* data collection, covert or overt, as problematic.

Research agendas

This brings me back to the question of research agendas and the related notion that one way to minimalize textual misrepresentation is to operate with entirely *explicit* research agendas. Covert taping necessarily excludes the researched from both involvement in the setting of the research agenda and from engagement in the representation of the information obtained. However, when we extend condemnation of clandestine data collection to clandestinity of research agenda the issue becomes more problematic. It is impossible to be entirely open about exactly what data are being collected, since it is only at the stage of writing that the collection of memories, impressions, notes and recordings become 'data' by going on record. Anthropologists have thus correctly pinpointed the moment of representation as the crucial limitation to participant observation as methodology. While necessitating the constant negotiation of identity, agenda and relative status in which both researcher and researched share their assumptions and knowledge, it is only the researcher who represents and at the point of data construction not even the researcher can know the form this representation will take, nor what its final content or agenda will be. Analysis involves abstraction; it also involves making explicit much of what was only implicit while in the field. In this sense agendas operate at different levels of consciousness.

People had obviously wanted to know why I intended to live in their village for two years. They knew about universities and required research projects and many even had a vague idea about anthropology as the study of culture and tradition, with a preference for the exotic and primitive. In this respect they thought that I had not chosen the best place to study. I told them that I was interested in understanding when people spoke Spanish and when they spoke Quechua, that I wanted to learn Quechua, and that I wanted to try to understand their beliefs and everyday behaviours. They knew that I intended to write a book. On the one hand this provoked misgivings as to the implications of my categorizing them as 'other'. However my project was also seen as a gesture of solidarity and commitment, their customs and beliefs were not simply validated but also preserved and protected through my representation of them.

However it is noteworthy that I found the whole issue of drunken speech something that was difficult to deal with as an explicit item on my research agenda as it did not sit easily with the solidarity agenda. This difficulty goes beyond my own cultural prejudices about the intrusion on drunken behaviour, and beyond the methodological problems of collecting data during drinking sessions where the researcher is often necessarily as drunk as the researched.

The study of drunken speech confronted me very directly with the problem of how to set explicit research agendas when researching the workings of power. Such research involves the observation not only of the 'powerless' but also of the 'powerful'. But who were the powerful and who the powerless? How can a researcher explicitly define such relations if they are not sure how power works, nor along which axes it is going to occur? In one sense all these people were powerless in the macro-context of the state and of western capitalism. However they did not experience themselves as equally powerless in the kinds of interactions which I was experiencing with them, and that applied equally to their relationships to me as to each other. It was particularly in drunken interaction that open challenges and negotiation of position took place.

As I mentioned, the question of who said what to whom and when became increasingly problematic as my understanding of power and identity developed. The more I understood of their categorization process, the more their discrete identities broke down. This is not to say that everything dissolved into an undifferentiated mass of relativistic positions in which power became a meaningless category; quite the reverse. People were very aware of their positioning despite the fact that this positioning was not stable. Such positioning also depended on the level at which the issue was approached, whether at the local or the supra-local level.

My own position was ambivalent in this sense. As anthropologist/ researcher I was obviously a powerful outsider. But that was not the only aspect of my identity, and certainly not the only one to which the people reacted. It was always there as an option and was often brought home to me when I did not behave in ways compatible with the other identities on offer to me. On one occasion when I refused a drink from a woman with whom I had formed a close and intimate friendship, she quite explicitly informed me that she would always treat me with respect but that I had changed and she no longer felt the same affection for me. However, in many ways I became part of the insider group – often consciously used by them in an advocacy role to contact other outsiders such as the foreign priest, or other *gringos*. On other occasions I was identified with a particular insider position in negotiations among themselves, – as godparent, as family member, as a woman.

My methodological problem was thus how to record the open negotiation of status and agenda implicit in participant observation. To use the tape recorder openly emphasised this particular way of putting statements on the record. It also enhanced my identity as researcher and outsider and thus made the occasion more formal and explicit challenges to authority and status (mine and other people's) less appropriate and therefore less likely to occur. However, without this material from the drinking sesions, recorded or remembered via more *ad hoc* methods, I could not have understood much about language and power in this community and I would have thus been unable to pursue my primary research agenda.

This agenda, the investigation of the relationship between language and power, was very difficult to communicate openly as it holds meaning in relation to my particular intellectual and political concerns. Their understandings of the relationship between language and power are quite different to mine. My informants depicted real power as lying outside the community – in the state and in the animate landscape which embodies supernatural power. The practices by which they attempted to negotiate authority and status locally are only effective and meaningful because they take place in the wider political and sociohistorical context and because they essentially involve an appeal to these sources of power that exist outside their community.

My explanatory frameworks make it possible for me to say that their lack of autonomy and hence their powerlessness in some senses arise from a failure to recognise that such power does not *necessarily* exist outside their sphere of direct influence and that their continuing representation of power in this way actually functions to maintain their position of powerlessness. Their analysis is different. Peru is experiencing economic collapse (inflation was 6,000 per cent in 1989) and a bloody guerrilla war. Real power in the Andes today is the power of the gun, and the power of the US dollar, military power, organised insurgency and counter-insurgency. Their positioning of power outside the community is a perfectly valid statement on their part that refers to the extent to which they experience themselves, as social actors, controlled by an outside and oppressive society, of which they are somehow no longer a part.

It is important to note that the centrality of the particular nature of concepts of power and identity which I now use in writing about Ocongate and by extension bilingualism, emerged from the process of analysis as I slowly worked to clarify the issues that were of central importance to the people I was working with. Thus although I set the agenda on power and language use, they defined their experience of power. However this is not the same as saying that they agreed I should research on these topics, or that my primary *research* aim was ultimately relevant to them.

It could be argued that if I want to look at the negotiation of power and identity I should do so in my own culture or in a situation in which I am more closely implicated in the subordinate position – in an examination of gender, for example. I did indeed feel more able to talk about power and control in the context of my subsequent work on gender relations, which I carried out on a second field trip in 1987. I think this was because my female gender was perceived as at least comparable if not exactly similar to that of the women I talked to in Ocongate. This point of identification made it easier for them to take an active interest in my position, to enquire about my experience and to make comparisons.

However, I would stress that gender identity draws on multiple masculinities, femininities and sexualities which hold social meaning through the ways in which they cross-cut the axes of class, ethnicity and age discussed on pp. 77–8. To say that I was identified as a woman is to present a very reductive version of how I was perceived and no account at all of how my experience and concept of womanhood fitted with theirs. I could not have begun to interpret their experience and representation of gender without making some attempt to understand their experience and representation of class, ethnicity and age.

Furthermore, to argue that only those in subordinate roles can appropriately research into particular power relations is to ignore the politics which govern the possibility for producing and distributing such work. Historically I am obviously implicated in the power relations of this Ocongate community not just as anthropologist, although my status as an academic is very important, but also as a member of a western colonial state. Their awareness of themselves as colonized poeple makes the issue of power a relevant one for research. The fact that it should be me and not them doing the research takes us back to the desire for empowering research and it leads me to (a) a discussion of the accessi-bility of research results and (b) an assessment of the degree to which the kind of research I did can be empowering.

ACCESSIBILITY AND LIMITS TO EMPOWERMENT

In many senses the research which I have described here is not comparable to the kind of variationist sociolinguistic research we describe in the introduction. I was not asking people to talk about particular topics while in reality listening out for a particular abstracted linguistic feature. These two levels could not be separated. Thus much of what I learnt and much of what I finally wrote about in my Ph.D. thesis was material that was already accessible to the researched, since they had told me about it. They told me about the two sources of external power, they explained their ambivalent historical identity, and if they did not explicitly link these concepts to their bilingual usage it is because it is a connection that has no immediate significance for their ways of thinking about themselves. It was not that I was looking for a logic in their lives which I could reveal to an academic community but not bother to share with them. Nor on this level did they have much respect for my expert knowledge. It was not something I had to demystify. I was often treated as a rather ignorant child, who was trying to learn their ways of being with no very obvious success.

Thus, although this research project did not set out to empower the researched, the use of participant observation as a basic method appears to go some way towards meeting the conditions for such research. This method is not directed towards 'natural' or objective data, and involves very close involvement with the researched both in the process of developing the detail of research agendas and in the construction of the salient identities of both researcher and researched. However the area in which this project underutilized the potential for empowerment was at the point of feedback. Much of the explicit knowledge given to me by the researched contained implicit assumptions which I analysed but did not directly share with them in the ways that Frazer has described in chapter 4.

Investigations of the structures of inequality implicitly hold an empowering agenda as such studies attempt to reformulate at the local level the conditions in which the researched coexist with each other, and in which they coexist with the researcher. The aim of such research is to reveal the processes through which hierarchy is constituted and the implicit assumptions that allow for its perpetuation and reproduction.

The results are published to challenge other positions taken within the academic community whose cumulative effect in turn and in time can inform policy decisions of very direct relevance to the researched. I am thinking here particularly of the policy areas of education, agriculture and health. While it would be naive to suppose that any study or set of studies will necessarily have any impact on the highly political sphere of policy making, it is also true to say that if empowerment results from disentrenchment of positions by revealing their political contingency then such research can indirectly feed back to the researched. The point appears particularly salient in a country such as Peru where intellectuals have considerable political influence and where the very nature of society and of the state is being openly challenged and questioned. Such indirect feedback is, however, more akin to our earlier definitions of advocacy than empowerment which must essentially involve the active participation of the researched.

Published data from my research was used by local people on one occasion, although without my prior knowledge. A Quechua/Spanish bilingual radio station in Cusco used excerpts from an article published in a relatively accessible journal, to discuss the relationship between bilingualism and language planning (Harvey 1987b). These popular radio stations, run by and for local communities, are very good channels for a wider feedback of research findings that both give control of representation to the people themselves and provide greater accessibility through use of an oral rather than written channel. This is one area which I think could usefully be explored in future projects and which might provide a way of addressing the fundamental question of power and hierarchy which informed the research project. However, the feedback is still at one remove. The people of Ocongate do not have a radio station and the material was used by the more urban populations of Cusco, even though these were Quechua speaking grass-roots organisations.

Many anthropologists, especially in the USA, are beginning to experiment with representational forms that explicitly confront both the collaborative project that fieldwork necessarily entails and the conflicts that can arise from conflicting research agendas. The recent collaboration between the Kayapo people of Amazonia and western environmentalists provides a topical example and shows ways in which videos, TV, written media and record publication can be used to serve the agendas of several groups at once. While western TV presentation of the Amazonian Kayapo through the use of the pop-star Sting and his associates, might not be one that they endorse, they can be seen videoing their demonstrations against Amazonian development for their own purposes while at the same time using the power of the western media to gain support in Washington and put pressure on the World Bank for tighter controls on 'development' projects.

Despite the limits to the negotiation of agendas and the problem involved in the process of data construction when looking at power relations, I feel that the example of the use of radio indicates a way in which areas of mutual interest that inevitably arise from the research process can be explored further. For example I had many discussions with people about the status of the Quechua language. Many people felt that Quechua was inferior to Spanish, that it was merely a dialect while Spanish was a language. Even people who were fully literate in Spanish would tell me that Quechua was impossible to write down. My ability to read and write Quechua – albeit initially without understanding a word – was greatly admired. Their admiration of my skills in literacy went hand in hand with a deprecatory attitude towards themselves. They said that even if I spoke less fluently than them, I spoke a better, purer form – my Quechua came from books whereas they had merely picked theirs up. My discussion of these issues was not a planned part of the research but more systematic discussion could have addressed their interests and my own.

As I have already suggested, participant observation can reveal such points of mutual interest without the necessity of convening the kinds of groups mentioned in other chapters of this book. The community of researched may not easily be identifiable as a group in this way. However a recurring element in our case studies does appear to point to the usefulness of non-literary media for further discussion of those agendas which do emerge as salient for the researched.

In terms of sharing those analytical results that researchers would tend to privilege in their written accounts I believe that it may be possible to be more explicit with the researched about the wider field of social relations and the particular body of knowledge in terms of which research data is being interpreted as I did for example in my discussion with informants on the political relationship between languages and dialects. However this particular kind of knowledge may not be of interest to the researched. Thus while the researcher should try to open discussions on this level they may also have to accept that there is a limit to the extent to which the researched are willing to collaborate in meeting the researcher's agenda for empowerment. Empowerment as defined by the researcher may not be an option they always want to consider, or one that they find relevant. Thus while I was looking at the constitution of hierarchy at the local level, their concern was primarily with the ways in which outside power acted on them. This was not a topic on which I could inform them.

A final anecdote illustrates that as researchers we also have to respect that the researched do not always want our 'knowledge'. I believe that we should strive to make it available but not thus assume that it will be acted upon. There was a Dutch doctor working in the village when I first arrived and he told me about an experiment that he had done in a small community. He had taken several water samples, from the ditch, the river, etc., and one sample of boiled water. These were placed in turn under the microscope and people were invited to look and see for themselves that the boiled water was purer and thus more suitable for drinking. An old woman had looked carefully at all the samples, thought about it for a while and then asked him which had been the dirtiest. When he pointed to the glass of ditch water she drank it down defiantly and declared that she had been drinking that for the last sixty years and was not going to stop now.

All cultures develop survival strategies in the face of their particular historical and political circumstances. The people I worked with were in fact very astute about the relationship between their powerlessness and the impact of colonialism and western economic and cultural hegemony. I make this final point simply to emphasise that empowering research must be directed as much at the political consciousness of the powerful as of the powerless – in this case in sharing the research results with people in Europe and the USA as well as with the Peruvians.

I have thus argued that in this particular research project there were serious limitations to the possibility of empowerment. To understand how people use historically established meanings to render their contemporary world meaningful is, I believe, an important task. The conflicts that emerge in drunken interaction reveal the ways in which social power and authority are distributed. It is important to remember that it is the drunks themselves who reveal the contingent nature of such power through their ability to challenge its legitimacy and field of appropriate application. The words and actions of drunks demonstrate that it is through normative discourse and social convention that societies and selves are constituted as integrated and natural entities. Drunks may not appear to have the social power to undermine such norms and conventions but by confronting them they reveal the artifice of social life and allow the imagination of alternative forms of social order. It is in this sense that drunkenness is experienced as empowering by drinkers.

We might not recognise drunkenness as empowering, yet we have to ask how it is that the knowledge generated by research can empower in more effective ways. My research was based on the premise that my informants understood very well what it means to be powerless. Local practice is a response to this disadvantaged social position, and a response that does not appear to offer a direct challenge to the wider forces of domination. Yet this response is not based on ignorance. My informants were not prevented from possessing and using expert knowledge through lack of knowledge, but because social conditions do not allow them to operate as experts. Furthermore they are aware that researchers do have this power and could therefore act for them. Indigenous populations are increasingly demanding that anthropologists *should* operate in advocacy roles, but unlike our earlier discussion of advocacy, the agendas are set by them, and are often stated as a precondition of the research being carried out at all.

NOTES

1 This research was supported by the Social Science Research Council and the University of London and was presented as a Ph.D. in Social Anthropology to the London School of Economics. The field research to which this chapter refers was carried out for a period of two years from June 1983 to September 1985.

2 Peru's major political divisions are at the level of departments. These are subdivided into provinces which are in turn subdivided into districts. Ocongate is a district capital in the Province of Quispicanchis, Department of Cusco.

3 The *puna* is the highest inhabitable ecological zone of the Andes, starting at the upper limit of corn production at *c*. 3,500 metres.

4 Bronislaw Malinowski (1884–1942) held the first Chair in Social Anthropology at the London School of Economics. He wrote seven monographs on the Trobriand Islands where he was stranded during the Second World War, and developed a particular theoretical approach to the analysis of this material, known as Functionalism. His better known works include: *Argonauts of the Western Pacific* (1922), *Crime and Custom in Savage Society* (1926), *The Sexual Life of Savages in North Western Melanesia* (1929) and *Coral Gardens and their Magic* (1935).

4

TALKING ABOUT GENDER, RACE AND CLASS

Elizabeth Frazer

INTRODUCTION

The project discussed here was an investigation into the ways teenage girls from different socioeconomic backgrounds understood gender, race and class relations, and how they negotiated a feminine identity and came to terms with the problems of femininity in contemporary British culture. The research was undertaken in the framework of recent British sociology of youth and gender – and was intended to be an exploration of the material and ideological processes by which young people take up a social and cultural identity and arrive at a particular position in the socioeconomic class structure.[1] I particularly focused on the processes by which girls and women are compelled to negotiate the options of marriage, motherhood and domestic work, and how they deal with violence and sexual oppression.

The data I shall present and discuss in this paper consist of transcriptions and analysis of discussions with seven groups of teenage girls, each with seven to nine members. I shall concentrate upon two specific groups, where events developed in ways that are particularly relevant to the concerns of this book. The groups met weekly during one school term (and in some cases two) for sessions which consisted of tea and biscuits, discussion on a variety of topics, games, drama, and exercises in group work and communication. By sociologists' criteria of social class based on occupation, the groups fell into three clearly distinct categories. There was a mixed age (14 to 16) and racially mixed (Afro-Caribbean, Black British, Turkish, white British and Irish) group from a London inner-city youth project. These girls' parents' and carers' occupations included kitchen assistants, factory workers, cleaners, part-time shop assistant, van driver. Their racial identities are self-ascribed – that is, I am employing the terminology they commonly used in talking about themselves and their friends. There were three groups from an Oxfordshire single-sex comprehensive school: two of 14-year-olds (fourth-formers) and one of 17-year-olds (upper sixth-formers). Two of these groups each included one Black girl (one Afro-Caribbean and one Kenyan), otherwise the members were white. Their parents' and carers' occupations included secretaries, plumber, police officers, nurses, midwife, master butcher, cabinet maker, night porter. Finally there were three groups (one third year, 13-year-olds, one lower sixth, 16-year-olds, and one upper sixth, 17-year-olds) from an Oxfordshire single-sex Headmistresses' Conference public school. Their parents included barristers, landowners, managers of various professional companies, stud manager, stock broker, army officers, QC, and farmers (the largest number being landowners and farmers).

In this chapter I shall first discuss my choice of method and research design, and the process of data construction and interpretation in the fieldwork; then talk about two aspects of the data which fit the criterion (with which I began) of 'democratic research'; and finally consider this work in the light of our subsequent discussions of research and empowerment.

SOCIOLOGICAL RESEARCH METHODS

Sociologists have used a variety of methods to discover how young people themselves understand and make sense of their economic, cultural and social situations, and how they negotiate the constraints and opportunities facing them, how they rationalise their choices and destinies, how they 'take up' a social identity and situation. In-depth interviews and questionnaires based on traditional survey methods have been used. At the point of writing, though, many sociologists in this field depart from traditional empiricist qualitative and quantitative analysis and present transcriptions of respondents' words with the intention of letting their voices be heard fully. This focuses interest on the ways young people themselves understand and conceptualise their situations.[2] Ethnography, the method of anthropology, has also been used, often in combination with interviews and survey methods, to observe, record and analyse patterns of political, passionate, economic and other social interactions and relations between persons, and to investigate the rules, norms, meanings and symbolism governing these interactions and relations.[3]

My experience in youth work and reading of critical literature on social science methods meant that making the transition to 'researcher' was problematic and anxiety-provoking for me. I was used to my interactions with young people being guided by educational aims, and led by their needs and interests, within the framework of the youth project. Being a researcher had unpleasant overtones of being dispassionate and disinterested (which also suggests *un*interested), of being manipulative (one might be interested and involved, or led by their needs – but only so as to obtain the data required for the research), and of perforce (by virtue of the logic of the social sciences) taking a spuriously objectivist view of the data. These doubts were not eased by a head teacher who told me that he was very reluctant to give any more researchers access to his school, because the school never seemed to benefit.

These doubts have not, of course, been ignored by professional sociologists. There is a good-sized literature on research ethics. And there have been critical developments from within sociology itself. One of these is the reflexive sociology we mentioned in the Introduction, which I will be discussing further. Another is the feminist critique of sociology.

Ethics and sociology

Sociologists, like other social scientists, recognise the potentially exploitative and damaging effects of 'being researched on'. A first concern is with the effect of the 'social scientific knowledge' constructed in research. Scientific and academic knowledge can have a central place in the social world and especially in the definitions and understandings of policy-makers and executives. Sociologists correlate sociological variables like income, ethnicity, criminality or deviance, patterns of parenting, and educational attainment. There is a danger that observation of, say, low academic achievement by some particular group of children can feed *expectations* of low achievement, and therefore absence of encouragement, challenge and stimulation in school. Social scientists therefore have long been urged to take care in the reporting and presentation of research findings – especially taking great care with the construction of putative explanations out of correlations (BSA 1982).

Second, there is the controversy about the acceptability of covert research, and other methods which rely on respondents not having an accurate idea of what is going on – we have discussed these issues and given some examples of such research in our introductory chapter. There have been vigorous debates about this in sociology (Bulmer 1982, Dingwall 1980, Homan 1980). Arguments in favour of posing as an ordinary member of the congregation in a church or as a homosexual voyeur in public places where sexual encounters occur are based on the fact that access to these settings as a sociologist would be impossible (or, if not impossible, would significantly alter the events and states of affairs being observed), and that it is not the case that real harm is done to the people observed. Arguments against have frequently rested on the value of the autonomy of the individual and of privacy, and on the belief that invasions of privacy and autonomy are intrinsically harmful. The integrity of the profession of sociology has also been marshalled – if it becomes widely known that sociologists snoop around public lavatories watching homosexuals, or pretend to be religious worshippers when they are not, then the profession will come into disrepute, access to settings will be more likely to be denied to overt and honest researchers in the future, and so on. These are instrumentalist arguments for ethics – we discussed other examples of these arguments in the Introduction. It is notable, too, that they are implicitly individualistic, trading on concepts like rights, autonomy and privacy. Others see it somewhat differently, though, stressing that the value of sociological knowledge and research has to be argued with all respondents, that the worth of sociological enquiry has to be established and accepted by the society in which the research is done. Any research which does not engage respondents to this extent is bad research (Dingwall 1980).

These criticisms mesh with the methodological critique of positivism we discussed in the Introduction. Insisting on the moral status of persons, the unacceptability of treating them as externally observable atoms, and the unacceptability of producing accounts of people's action which bear no resemblance to their own accounts, flows into the hermeneuticist insistence that 'social reality' is, at least partly, constituted by actors' own conceptions of it and their acts. When taken to an extreme this position can deny the privileged status of social scientific accounts of the world at all. But even if we stop far short of this view, the insistence that the participants' own accounts must be part of the scientific, means that researchers must engage with respondents in a way that is at odds with the ideal of pure and uncontaminating observation. The insistence that respondents must accept the aims and practices of the research and be aware of its implications flows into a reflexive awareness of the status of discourses of social science in constructing the complex reality we inhabit. It denies the neutrality of facts; and flows into the anti-positivist emphasis on the constructed nature of data, the theory-ladenness of observation, and the necessity for an explanation which goes behind the superficially 'observable' statistical correlations of the empirical world.

Feminist criticism of sociology

Among the academic disciplines sociology has been an important focus for the development of feminist knowledge, research and politics since the mid-1960s. However, in the process feminism has launched a far-reaching and sustained attack on many aspects of sociological theory and practice. Not all sociological programmes are equally antipathetic to feminism – some, such as symbolic interactionism and ethnomethodology, with their emphasis on the constructed and emergent nature of social reality and consciousness, and the constructed nature of knowledge, have been useful and influential in feminism. Feminists have also met more orthodox sociologists on their own ground, and argued that in the interests of scientificity sexist bias must be redressed. But, equally, no existing sociological programme meets all the needs of a feminist epistemology and methodology – empiricism is insufficiently sensitive to the constructed nature of social reality, identity and knowledge, while symbolic interactionism and ethnomethodology are insufficiently sensitive to coercion and power in social life.

Feminist sociologists have mounted a familiar attack on the objectifying and manipulative stance of traditional social science with its emphasis on disinterestedness, objectivity, and value-freedom. The starting point for this criticism lies precisely in feminist politics and the principle that you (as researcher or not as researcher) cannot be disinterested or value-free in the study of situations in which oppression and inequality are structured. Feminism is a politics of the oppressed, and feminist researchers must identify with the oppressed and have an interest in putting research and science at the service of the oppressed. Similarly feminism as a politics is engaged in the destruction of sexism, heterosexism, and gender inequality of all kinds. This informs the feminist scientist's choice of research problem and her sociological analysis as well as her research method – the traditional pretence that the categories of science, and the direction of research, are dictated by a logic of scientific discovery which is somehow internal to the scientific process itself, is rejected (Harding 1986: 209–215).

The immediate upshot of this is that feminist methods depart from traditional scientific methods in significant ways. Janet Finch's reflections on interviewing women, and Ann Oakley's, are good representatives of this line of thought (Finch 1984; Oakley 1981). Their point is that as a woman interviewing women one's stance cannot be detached – the dynamics of relations between women produce a shared creation of meaning, an exchange, an understanding. This presumably might be the case between men too, and it would be as well if male researchers were to explore this more – as some now do (see Morgan 1981). Oakley pours scorn on traditional norms of interviewing which seek to minimise researcher contamination of the data, and which enjoin the interviewer not to be drawn into any discussion with the respondent, to deflect questions. When she was interviewing women about the transition to motherhood she was asked 878 direct questions, including 'how do you cook an egg for a baby?', 'how long should you wait for sex after childbirth?' and even 'which hole will the baby come out of?'. She invites us to consider the possibility of responding to any of these enquiries with a shrug, or with 'Well, right now your opinions are more important than mine' as recommended in one textbook for interviewers (Oakley 1981).

These feminist arguments are congruent with the ethical debates examined earlier, but proceed from a different starting point – rather than the universalistic principles of humanism, the specific standpoint of feminist politics. Subsequently, feminists have developed the idea of 'standpoint epistemology'. The point here is that from different positions in a social structure different processes and relations can be *seen*. Feminists have written much about the invisibility of women's work in industrial societies. On the one hand they criticise male science for having rendered it invisible; on the other they have described and analysed it and made it visible as knowledge. But its invisibility until now is not an accident, or the result of small-minded ill will on the part of men. Rather, from the traditional sociological perspective – a male perspective – the world is constituted by classes, families, firms, status groups and so on. Those who inhabit this realm – the capitalist, the director, the factory worker, the parent – do so from a base of the body which must be reproduced and cared for. Because it is possible for men to neglect and ignore these reproductive and maintaining processes, the sociological stance has been able to cut this conceptual space loose from its material base and treat it as *sui generis*, reify it. The woman sociologist, though, will find this much harder to do, as she attends seminars and teaches classes between shopping, cooking, picking up the children and being absent from work because of children's illness (Smith 1986). Just as Oakley and Finch emphasise that a woman interviewing a woman cannot take up a disinterested stance (and therefore can't do good orthodox sociology) so these later theorists emphasise that to women the material bodily base of the sociological world is visible and constraining and insistent. In both cases the orthodox stance and ideal is shown to be partial, biased, based on a particular set of subjective and political interests.

There are obvious and complex issues here, with what can look like an essentialist assumption that all women share the feminine standpoint and all men the masculine. Discussing these fully would take at least a chapter by itself. I shall make only a couple of brief comments. First, it must be, and has been, possible that women sociologists as well as men are capable of overlooking the bodily base of social reality; we cannot take it for granted that all women are on the same side here, nor that all men are blithely ignorant of reproduction and maintenance of bodily being. Nevertheless, it has been feminist theory that has instigated this critique. It has been an influential development for empirical and theoretical sociologists who are conscious of the abstractly disembodied status of sociological categories and roles; and are concerned to redress the balance (e.g. Connell 1987). Again, the methodological implications push us in a familiar direction. The 'facts' of social science turn out to be constructs. So the process by which they are constructed must be attended to. The objective disinterested stance is not possible – the knowledge and the knower are bound up together, and this must be acknowledged. The social, political, passionate and economic relations between researcher and researched shape the data.

Action research and new paradigm research

The programme of action research has become very familiar in education, youth work and community work, and in development and economics. It first encompasses a recognition of the principle that research, the discovery of information that is necessary and interesting and appropriate, is a good and beneficial thing for people to do, and can transform the frequently negative and unpleasant experience of education. 'Doing a project' on tropical rainforests can be as boring, stultifying and alienating as rote learning of tables; but finding out something that you really need and want to find out about for your life – drawing up a proposal for the youth project, or doing 'market research' for an adventure playground (that is, doing a 'real' project) can bring the notions of knowledge, facts, skills, properly alive. Doing research about the needs and worries of the population of the neighbourhood can be beneficial to a community association, both in the sense of bringing knowledge which can potentially make the association more effective, and in the sense of being a politicising, educational and bonding experience for the people who participate.

Action research has also played an honourable part in many development projects, and is especially connected with the appropriate technology movement, where local people join with agency experts to research and design and institute co-operatives, community organisation, production and commercial enterprises, agricultural, medical and educational improvements, for themselves. This kind of research project destroys the traditional sharp demarcation between research to establish needs, and the subsequent policy decision and execution to answer those needs. The first principle is that needs must be identified *and answered* – the second stage cannot be the optional extra it always has been (think of the many dust-gathering royal commission reports and recommendations to the British government). The second principle is that needs cannot simply be diagnosed from outside by an expert – the model of the orthodox doctor who tells you what's wrong with you must be rejected. The community members themselves must participate in the diagnosis, and also their knowledge of their own community means that they must be able to judge what is and what is not possible by way of remedy or improvement.

The methodological underpinnings of action research, together with insights from various therapeutic and counselling traditions and from group dynamics have been made explicit, mainly by social psychologists, under the heading of 'new paradigm research' (Reason and Rowan

1988). Like action research the new paradigm is intended to be explicitly liberationist, and has been constructed as a critique of the 'old' positivist paradigm. Its purpose is multi-faceted: first to involve people in the diagnosis of and remedy for their own needs and problems (where that is the research aim); second to refrain from treating persons as objects; third to avoid exploiting them; fourth to ensure that research is not put at the service of oppressive policy; fifth to refrain from deceiving them; and sixth, to refrain from reifying 'facts', and indeed persons, into immutable things and to recognise the transformability of social reality.

Many distinct programmes – from encounter group work and other active therapies, to Illuminative Evaluation (a programme of self-assessment for professionals), to the use of group dynamics studies for professional teams and groups – can be gathered under this heading, as well as more straightforwardly academic research methods like the one we are developing in this book. Common to all is the rejection of the distinction between the discovery of facts and normative policy making (that is, the rejection of the traditional positivist paradigm for social science), attention to the liberationist possibilities of research, and the insistence that people should be party to the research process.

A notable, and extremely influential, example of research in such a paradigm is Alain Touraine's work on social movements (1981, 1983). He calls his research method 'sociological intervention' – social actors (in this case, members of social movements) are the analysts of their own action. Again, the research and response distinction is collapsed – traditional survey research describes a situation, and then a response to it may or may not be put in train. In research into social movements this model is quite inappropriate (if, indeed, it is anywhere really appropriate). The situations in which social movements arise are not static, and the social movements themselves are not static. But while on the move, participants can reflect on what they are doing. The sociologists act as facilitators for this process. During the 1980s, doing some research with Solidarity, the Polish workers' movement, sociologists worked with small groups. Each group had two sociologists – one to facilitate and act as an agent or enabler of the self-analysis, the other to act as analyst – to introduce hypotheses and accounts which are discussed, accepted or rejected, or modified, by the group. The groups' acting on these analyses is part and parcel of *doing* the analysis. This aspect of the work Touraine calls 'permanent sociology'.

'DEMOCRATIC RESEARCH'

The upshot of my musings and readings in methodology before I began fieldwork were these conclusions: first, that if I did good youth work I would not be exploiting or alienating the girls; and, second, that doing good youth work was not incompatible with doing good research. On the first point, it is interesting that Janet Finch has argued that girls and women are not alienated by 'being researched' – the age-old problem of 'rapport' which haunts traditional handbooks for interviewers seems not to be a problem at all when a woman talks to other women about any aspect of womanhood (Finch 1984). Certainly my own experience bears this out. The second point, however, needs more discussion. The status of the data obtained is far from the ideal (and, as has been argued, mythical and unobtainable) of the positivist programme. My argument is that democratic research *methods* (ways of researching that refrain from treating persons as objects, refrain from misrepresenting or mystifying the research process) and non- or anti-positivist research *methodology* – a rejection of the absolute objectivity and the quantifiability of data – are tied up with one another. In what follows I am going to discuss the process of data construction and interpretation in my fieldwork, and the precise ways in which I attempted to do 'democratic research'.

The notion of 'democratic research' with which I set out involved three principles – the principle of making room for the girls' own agendas to be fulfilled, the principle of properly checking that my interpretations of what they said agreed with their intentions, and the principle of feeding back the results of the research (whatever they might be) to them. I was taking action research and other varieties of 'new paradigm research' in which the 'data' is self-consciously con-structed by the participants or respondents themselves, as an ideal. My project fell far short of it however: the groups I worked with didn't have ready-made research agendas of their own and the project of working with them to find one (which obviously would have been possible) was ruled out by the constraints of time governing D.Phil. research in Britain. I was also constrained by my own preoccupation with theoretical questions, to do with the relation between language and reality, from which I did not want to be deflected. The girls certainly did have agendas, as was made clear by the alacrity with which they volunteered to participate in discussion groups – to talk, to spend time, have fun, discuss their problems. I shall also go on to discuss later the extent to which my aim of having the girls *agree* the data as constructed was not always fulfilled, and never fulfilled wholeheartedly. Nevertheless, even with this kind of 'failure', the principle of checking back means that researchers can try to avoid positive misrepresentation of respondents' positions.

The groups were discussion groups, based on a contract which meant that membership was closed, that members agreed to attend regularly, and keep confidentiality. In the sessions it was agreed that participants would listen supportively, discuss issues co-operatively (not competi-tively, as in debating), and would participate in the general activities and talk (not, for example, do their homework or have private chats). Obviously, it was my reseach project which brought the groups together, and discussions, which I started by posing a question or questions about a variety of topics to do with gender relations, were the centrepiece of sessions. My agenda, that is, was pre-eminent. However, girls (at this historical point) do undoubtedly want to talk about gender. And it was part of the contract that within the framework of the time, space and resources available the girls' own agendas could be fulfilled – we could discuss anything they wanted to discuss and do things they wanted to do.

This resulted in a variety of outcomes. It meant that different groups spent time talking about different topics. One group was very pre-occupied with family, and especially parental, relations, and we spent a whole session talking about that (I didn't record it). Two groups wanted to continue meeting in the school term following the completion of my data collection, so we continued meeting and did a photography project – producing an alternative photo-story magazine. Taking the girls' own agendas seriously not only means making space and allocating resources to major projects like this – it also involves attending to their needs in the micro-context of the group. There were tensions and clashes between members at times and these were discussed and acknowledged as part of the group process. Of course this depended on the girls telling me what was going on, or on my working it out for myself and asking.

Obviously this way of working has an effect on the data. It is incompatible with any research method which relies on the standardised administration of a closed schedule questionnaire which requires the minimum of 'interference' or 'researcher effect'. In these discussion groups I could in no circumstances absent myself from the process of data construction – I was a part of the group (and the most powerful member at that). Inevitably, what the girls said and how they said it was shaped by this context and my presence in it. For example, when I came to analyse the transcripts of the discussions I was very struck by how contradictory the girls were about various topics. This meant that it was impossible to report, as a scientific analyst, what any girl or group of girls believed about any particular issue (say, whether homosexuality is acceptable), or what their opinions on such a matter were. A closed schedule questionnaire, or even an in-depth interview, is more likely to elicit from respondents a unitary and articulated opinion, attitude or belief. The discussion group elicited, instead, an uncertain negotiation of alternative positions which were frequently unresolved. This is a function of the setting (as is the eliciting of a unitary opinion in conventional survey research). On the other hand, not *any* position was considered and discussed – overtly sexist or racist views are not voiceable in such a context: the norms of rational and co-operative discussion affect what can be said.

Checking my interpretations with the girls themselves was an attempted response to two problems. First is the problem of explanation – and the principle that in social research into people's behaviour and experience our explanations and theories must mesh with the concepts, categories and understandings employed by the people themselves. Survey research, as we have seen, can discover correlations between, say, people's educational attainment and their sexual behaviour. But the discovery of the correlation does not give us an explanation. It is tempting just to say, for instance, that girls with relatively low educational attainment, in the sense of examinations passed, will opt for single motherhood while still in their teens much more often (statistically speaking) than girls with O and A Levels. But just saying this leaves open the possibility that the mechanism by which this occurs *is* a mechanical one (analagous to the force of gravity). Or it may be a question of rational choice on the part of the girl herself. Or it may be a mixture of normative expectations by others, cultural norms and rules, socially specific forms of relations between boys and girls, socially specific sexual practices. However it is that girls end up behaving and acting in this way, a proper explanation of that sociological fact must take account of the girl's own reasons for acting as she does, the way she experiences the pressures and expectations that she is under, and the real concrete network of social relations she inhabits.

Second, and connected, is the necessity of avoiding misrepresentation of respondents. There is the obvious ethical and professional requirement that research data should be accurate. But also, and more complexly, a great deal of recent research into people's experience presents subjects as confused or mystified or self-contradictory. My own data includes instances of girls saying in one breath that the label 'slag' is oppressive and shouldn't be used about girls, and in the next breath calling each other slags. Or saying that lesbians are disgusting, and also saying that people's sexual lives are their own affair. There are problems with a common sociological response to this kind of data – which is to report that subjects are confused, mystified and unenlightened and that this is evidence for the power of ideology or the prevalence of false consciousness or cognitive dissonance. First there is the ever-present possibility that the 'contradiction' tells us more about the research context than about the person. Second, if people appear to be confused doesn't the researcher have a duty to check on why and how?

Obviously there are practical problems and issues with checking back. To begin with, if it is to be done it means that transcription and preliminary analysis has to be done from week to week while the fieldwork is going on. At least it has to be possible to go back to the respondents after analysis. In addition, asking people about apparent contradiction (even when softened with messages like 'I think I didn't understand properly ...') is potentially threatening and is only possible in circumstances where there is trust between researcher and respondents. An instance of checking back forms one of the case studies in this chapter. Feeding back the results of the research was more problematic in my project. In the end my attempts to feed back the results became incorporated into my own data construction, and were more like 'checking back' than 'feeding back'. That is, it was not the case that I 'did research', came to conclusions, and told the girls my conclusions. The reasons for this are, at least partly, epistemological, that is to do with the difficulty of construing the girls' talk as anything like factual data.

In what follows I am going to discuss the photo-story project and one exercise in checking back. I shall pay especial attention to the ways in which these improved the quality of the data I obtained, fulfilled the girls' own agendas, and to a certain extent involved them in the research that took them beyond being research objects. Finally, I shall assess them in light of the discussions of 'empowering research' we had which led up to the writing of this book.

PRODUCING A TEXT

The two groups of comprehensive school fourth-formers both wanted to continue meeting in the school term after the fieldwork was complete. They had particularly liked sessions in which we discussed popular culture, and when we talked about what activities the continuing groups could do, the possibility which most attracted them was to make an 'alternative' photo-story magazine. I suggested the two groups might join together for this (this would mean one meeting a week, instead of two for me) but they were keen to continue in their original small groups. As this was a complicated project which promised to be time-consuming, I got some help from among my friends and colleagues – one woman to work generally with each of the groups, and two women who knew about photography. These women all agreed to work with the girls as a good and useful experience – either for improving and thinking about their own work with teenagers in their own professional lives, or as a sort of 'voluntary youth work' experience.

We began by discussing commercial photo-stories and why we are critical of them. We then used the brainstorming method to come up with the elements of our alternative stories: this involved me writing absolutely every idea anyone came up with on a board, encouraging them to say out loud any idea they had. They were familiar with this technique as we had used it in various games and exercises before. It has many virtues: it encourages a free flow of ideas, and unconstrained use of the imagination; it values every idea equally as it emerges, and therefore encourages every member of the group to participate.

From this mass of material an outline story then emerged by a chaotic procedure of group discussion.

The subject matter of the two stories is interesting: they are about money (or rather the lack of it), boredom, sexual harassment, and economic exploitation. These stand in sharp contrast to the themes of photo-stories for girls, where if these issues arise at all they are likely to be resolved by *romance* which, unsurprisingly, is entirely absent from our alternative plots.

When we had our outlines we spent some time on improvisation of dialogue and character. The girls then had to work out roughly what was to be in each frame, and I prepared detailed 'shooting schedules'. We adults had costed the production of a twelve- or fourteen-page magazine which would give five A4 sides for each story, and we raised money from university students. A photographic company we wrote to, telling them about our educational project, donated film, paper and chemicals. The girls themselves arranged permission for our 'location work' – in a shop where one of them worked on Saturdays, and in a boatyard where some of them had holiday jobs. We used my house for domestic scenes. The photography was done in one go – each group with their helper and photography specialist taking a different route around their locations, and ending up in the local ice-rink where each group had some scenes to photograph.

In the next couple of weeks the film was developed and printed. We were able to use the school darkroom and nearly all the girls had an opportunity to do at least a little work in it. The most difficult thing was pasting up the pages (with already photo-copied and reduced versions of the prints), and writing the dialogue neatly in the balloons and making the stories run properly. We added some background information about the groups and some transcribed discussion about the project to complete the magazine. Some of the girls involved talked about the project in their English lesson, and we made an exhibition of the magazine, the photographs and so on for the school entrance hall.

This project is a good example of making space for the girls' own agendas, rather than my own. It answered their desire that their groups should continue to meet through the school year and that I should continue to act as a facilitator and enabler for them. Researchers frequently remark that they feel that participating in research itself does fulfil respondents' own agendas – it gives respondents an opportunity to talk at length to someone who really listens, and seems genuinely interested, to someone who asks intelligent questions; it raises their self-esteem; it sometimes means that they learn interesting things about what's going on in sociology or political science (Finch 1984). However, invariably these are seen as pleasant by-products of the research process, mere bonuses – their absence would in no sense vitiate the research project or the data obtained. Sometimes, emphasis is laid on the extent to which the fact that the respondents enjoy the research limits the damage that research naturally does (in the normal course of events, given normal models of the research process).[4]

On this view critics might draw a distinction between what was youth work and what was research in my dealings with these girls (and argue that the youth work is, sociologically speaking, irrelevant). However, I argue that the youth work was the *context* of the research, and this is no different for analytic purposes than a situation where research is the context of the research. It might be considered that where a researcher appears simply as a researcher, and interacts with informants, then the situation is all much more simple: what is going on is perfectly plain. However, it seems to me that this is not the case. A researcher always has to enquire exactly what role she is perceived as having – and this role will rarely be that of researcher *per se*.

This point is relevant to the debate about the ethics of covert participatory research (Bulmer 1982). One point made in this controversy is that in covert research researchers are 'playing a role', engaging in pretence, behaving in an inauthentic fashion, and that this is damaging – to their own integrity, to the integrity of the social situation in which they participate, and more prosaically, to the reputation of sociologists as professionals. This argument clearly implies that there is an 'authentic' role of researcher. It implies that researchers can be wholly honest about what they are doing (by contrast with covert researchers who are necessarily dissimulating and lying). But current theories of social identity and subjectivity, and the experience of doing research which has been reported by many women (and some men), disputes this. Our social identities (when we are researching, or doing anything else), are not unitary or simple. We are women, and researchers, and adults, and youth workers, holders of certain political principles, certain moral beliefs, and so on.

Following from this, first, is the point that being wholly open and honest about who we are and what we are doing is not quite such a straightforward matter if our relationships with respondents are to be any more than formal. In any case, social roles like that of 'researcher' are not clear and unambiguous. Researchers ask questions, but they have to do so in an unthreatening way with various politenesses which are likely to be drawn from other distinct cultural roles, like that of 'friend', or 'expert', or 'sympathetic listener'. So, second, the researcher, during fieldwork, and at the point of analysis and data construction, always has to ask herself how she is perceived and how she is behaving, and take account of that. I have to take account of my 'youth worker' role in this work (and the role of youth worker of course has elements of 'friend', and 'teacher' in it).

Further to these issues of identity, my research and that of the other contributors to this book focused on respondents' experience – in my case, of femininity. I was interested in looking at how the girls negotiated with images and standards of femininity, and how they tackled the problems of gender relations that face them. My point here is that such research cannot trade on a model which takes the facts to be out there in the world and the research process to be the observation of and recording of these facts. For experience, understanding and discourse are never complete, but are continuous and processual. The process of experiencing, understanding and talking about femininity continues in the research process itself, and is shaped by the research process just as it is shaped by school, family, the ice-rink, Saturday work, and all the other social contexts of the girls' lives.

I cannot in that case analyse the transcripts of the discussions I had in the first term's work with these girls, and treat the photo-story project as a completely separate post-script. I cannot discuss their experience and discourse of gender without discussing the photo-story. If the first term's work is 'data' then so is the photo-story. In this sense, whatever form the work we did under the heading of 'the girls' own agenda' took, it would have to be part of the research project itself. Their agenda is part of the research; and crucially, the research is part of their agenda. By this I mean that the fact that this group wanted to continue to meet together and work with me, and chose to work on a project like the photo-story (instead of any of the other number of things we could have spent the term doing) has to be part of my 'knowledge' of how these girls are. (They are imaginative, and energetic, and solid with each other. ...) But the fact that they were presented with the opportunity to work in this way is of course relevant: I haven't access to any 'pure, uncontaminated, objective' state of affairs which exists independently of the research. *The research* finds them to be imaginative, energetic and solid.

The research, further, elicited several *contrasting* accounts of gender relations from these girls – from the highly conventional, to the highly feminist. I cannot report any of them as matters of fact about the girls' perceptions, beliefs, experience or understanding, or attribute more authenticity to one rather than another. The photo-stories – especially the one about sexual harrassment – are clearly 'feminist', using feminist categories and analysis of girls' situation. These girls, like all the others in the project, routinely talked in a feminist way about the sexual double standard, unfairness in the family, problems in jobs and schooling. However, they also discussed boys they fancy, and talked about gender relations, marriage and so on, in the conventionally sexist ways that constantly make girls workers despair. The question which of these is the girls' 'true' view is an idle one. Their experience is complex, and the ways of apprehending it available to them from existing discourses are multiple. In my next case study I discuss this complexity and multiplicity of subjects' experience, and the role of the research in shaping this, in more detail.

CLASS, RACE AND CONTRADICTION

In one session I wanted to elicit from the girls what normative content the idea of femininity had for them, and I posed the question of how girls ought to behave at parties. The public school sixth-formers, in response to this, mentioned 'making an effort with dress', 'making an effort to talk to people', 'not being too boisterous', not being 'obvious' or 'flirting'. The discussion was a combination of the girls putting forward these rules and conventions straightforwardly *as* rules and conventions, and arguing about *whose* rules they were, whether they were fair, and what they implied about social relations in their culture.

At a pause I asked:

EF: What about in school? can you work out, you can imagine the possibility of somebody coming to the school who really didn't fit in, really broke, was disapproved of?

and after this point the conversation took an unexpected turn. They certainly could imagine such a person – if she 'wore white socks', or were 'called Sharon', or were Black, or failed to talk with the correct accent, or were foreign at all (not only Black), or were highly intelligent, or said 'toilet' instead of 'lavatory', or 'settee' instead of 'sofa' ... The list goes on and on. What was unexpected was that the girls in the group were becoming very upset, and when the session finally came to an end (and some members of the group had to leave to go to a lesson) some of those who were left burst into tears, and I had to stay with them for more than another hour doing my best to put them back together again and talking some more, in what I hoped was a constructive fashion, about the issues that had been so painful.

The transcript reveals that there were several things going on. First, the girls in this group wanted to dissociate themselves from what they perceived as the stupid snobbery and prejudices of many other girls in the school:

EF: why Sharon?

Arabella: oh it's just a name that some people

Kate: it's a name that a lot of people look down on

Sara: yes but I don't agree with that, I think that it's just people's individual opinions here, I think that half this form wouldn't take a second's notice, it's just the half with all their stupid prejudices that

Amy:	and what if she was Black?
Kate:	it's more than half who take notice

On the other hand, their own experience of class relations meant that they shared the same emotions and views that were prejudices in the others:

Kate:	but most of the people down in the working cl ..., well
Sara:	yes, just when we walk in, just because we're [name of school] girls if we walk into [nearest town] when we're wearing uniform
Annabel:	yes, they're shouting
Sara:	tripping us up
Kate:	we've got these people with milk bottles threatening to smash them in our faces

and:

Kate:	did anyone throw stones at your horse when you're riding past?
Arabella:	throw stones at your bike, throw ...
Kate:	I mean I don't know if the snobs' views of the lower class are as bad as the lower class view of the snobs

One member of the group, who is from the United States, was consistently impatient with the others' dilemma and very challenging:

Annabel:	I don't like white socks
Amy:	because you find them impractical is not the reason

and:

Amy:	then some people go, well yes I know a Black person, she's really nice
Annabel:	but some of us don't know a Black person
Amy:	yes and I feel very sorry for you

and scathing about other girls in the school:

Amy:	I do hate Sloanes, I still hate them
Annabel:	you can still hate them, but you can't hate the individual people, I mean do you remember in [name of school house] you put up this big argument, 'I hate Sloanes' but you see the thing is here, horrible as it may be, this is a Sloane school, there are Sloane people, and you cannot make a wide ...
Amy:	well I don't know, that's not true
Annabel:	you can hate the attitude, but you can't hate the people, I don't know

106

Kate: you can't hate the people underneath the Barbours and
the Hunter wellies

On the one hand was the girls' knowledge of class conflict, guilt about
their own upper-class status and their families' real wealth and power
(and, incidentally, a fear that all these are really threatened by incipient
socialism!), and a consequent real fear and dislike of the 'lower classes'.
This structural reality of social life makes class conflict (waged in
mundane but nevertheless frightening ways from both sides) inescapable.
This is an unpalatable fact about life. On the other hand, an available
and possible softener, or way of negotiating this reality, is to emphasise
the importance of people (not class). Individuals are important; indeed
they are everything. Some individuals have ridiculous prejudices and
class attitudes, it is true: there are nasty upper-class people and nasty
lower-class people – but most people are nice. And if they are nasty it's
really because of ignorance:

Sara: most of the people who are really snobby around here
are the people who haven't got, they don't know anyone
who wears white socks, that's why, it's just ignorance

Class hatred as such is therefore simply illogical and impossible: there
are *people* under the Barbours and Hunters, and presumably under the
white socks too.

The transcript shows that it was this conflict, between individualism
and class analysis, which so thwarted and frustrated the girls. The
negotiation, after all, does not work – and certainly at the level of their
own experience it doesn't work, because they genuinely feel, and know,
two contradictory things. The conceptual conflict had also, of course,
manifested itself as conflict between group members, and it would have
been quite wrong not to acknowledge this. I asked the girls if they would
like to listen to the tape and read the transcript, and with some
trepidation, they agreed.

In preparation for that session I 'extracted' conflicting statements
from the transcripts and put them on cards. For example:

1 (a) My personal identity, life, my history and my future are only
to do with my individual self, my talents, drives and desires.
  (b) My personal identity, life, my history and my future are tied
up with my membership of social groups, such as class, race
and gender.

2 (a) People who are very class conscious (and e.g. sneer at white
socks) are too concerned with appearances and don't pay
enough attention to what individual people are really like.

(b) People who are very class conscious (and e.g. sneer at white socks) are only reacting to the reality of class hostility in our society.

3 (a) Hostility between classes is just like the rivalry between schools. It is based mostly on ignorance and prejudice.

(b) Hostility between classes can't be broken down just by members of different classes getting to know one another. There is much more at stake than there is in inter-school rivalry.

These conflicting statements are my interpretation (and 'translation' into 'propositional' language) of what the girls themselves said in the course of the discussion. As my interpretation of 'what the girls said' they rely on my knowledge of what members of this culture can say about class and class relations - I have understood their utterances as instances or articulations of familiar and institutionalised discourses of class, viz. individualism, class as constructing one's social identity, and class as a relation of exploitation and therefore hostility.

At the beginning of the feedback session we discussed the technique of 'glossing' – of reading and interpreting text, making its implications explicit, and inferring the presuppositions which underpin it, in the way that I had in extracting the propositions. In the session we concentrated on two particular extracts from the transcript – one from early on where the girls were arguing about who says and what is meant by 'girls shouldn't try too hard at parties', and a later part where they were circulating round and round the vexed topic of 'white socks'.

Several things happened in this session. First, and most important, the girls were able to clarify 'what they meant' when they said something, or what they thought others meant:

Amy: yes, at the top of page 5, Sara's bit, I, in the thing of when she said 'I don't disapprove of them so much ... ' it struck me, it was more sort of she was feeling sorry for them, but then, is she? or is she, or are all of us making allowances, because, really do these sort of people *want* to know, people who are whatever, dress, white socks, everything, I think that you can say 'well, they don't know anyone, so like that, so really it's OK cos they just you know, they've got a silly idea in their heads' but I think it's deeper than that, I think it's that they don't want to know anyone like that so really, they are to blame

Sara: yeah, I suppose some people want to remain ignorant, but then again you have to feel sorry for them because they want to remain ignorant
(*laughter*)

And the argument was able to go on but in a calmer atmosphere. Thus, there was a reconciliation at the level of the group dynamics. However, often in the course of the discussion I felt that the confusion of the original session was only being reproduced, and at those points I would put the propositions I had prepared in for discussion. In response to the second set quoted above they said:

Amy: yes that's very true [i.e. statement 2 (a) – EF]

Kate: well yes that's extremely true

Sara: my immediate reaction to that though my immediate reaction to that is not um a yes or a no, it's a why should there be class hostility in the majority when so many minorities from different classes get along perfectly well

Amy: no my reaction is, you see I don't think they're reacting to it I think they're creating it

Kate: yeah, it's because people sneer at white socks that you get class hostility

Sara: no, I don't think they're creating it themselves I think they're making bigger what has already been created by their class

EF: talking about white socks like that *reproduces* cl ...

Amy: but not just reacting, I mean that's the easy way out, 'oh well, that's the way the world is, I just react to it'

EF: OK

There was no reconciliation of ideas and commitments, though, either between the group members (for example Amy and Sara) or within group members (in this extract Kate is still veering between denial of and recognition of class relations). What this single session did was make explicit where the tension lay and exactly what the tension was.

This example, like others in my data, makes clear that there is not one, authentic, true 'opinion' or 'view' that good research can elicit from subjects. Human experience is ambiguous, and for any individual the ambiguity is rooted in the variety of discourses available for making sense of our lives, relations and reactions. All of the contrasting and contradictory things the girls said and felt about class, after all, are well institutionalised in the culture. Nevertheless, contradiction and conflict generate tension, and in discussions of the sort that people typically have with researchers who are conducting in-depth interviews, or like the ones here, contradiction and conflict are made plain.

Annabel: one of the teachers asked me if I was enjoying this [the research project – EF], and I said, 'Yeah, it's fine, it's OK', but that was before we did this, and this has been the *most* interesting ... studying that conversation has taught me so much about myself

EMPOWERING RESEARCH

To end I want to discuss two questions raised by our conception of 'empowering research': the question of the relation between knowledge and power; and that of the relationship between my 'standpoint' and that of the girls.

The coincidence of knowledge and power has made its way into critical common sense following Foucault's analysis. According to him, in the modern era the maintenance of an unequal, and, for many a repressive, social order no longer relies on fixed hierarchical social relations where, say, peasants are tied to landlords in something like a property relation; nor does it rely on the physical coercion which structured the early capitalist period. Instead people are constrained in social roles by regimes of truth which define them as marginal, or deviant, or sick, or healthy or authoritative. In this analysis, then, knowledge positions us in the social order, and it is knowledge that is at stake in social struggles – power engenders resistance, from which we may conclude (although Foucault is vague on this process) that knowledge engenders oppositional knowledge.

The research discussed in this chapter focused on the construction and experience of gender – an aspect of social identity much contested in the modern era when attempts to polarise masculinity and femininity and settle men and women into strictly defined gender roles have constantly had to struggle against feminism (the major and most powerful opponent of the dominant gender ideology) and other oppositional discourses like some versions of psychoanalysis – which unsettle, or deconstruct, the gender categories. One way of looking at the data from this project is to see it as a rehearsal and re-rehearsal by groups of teenage girls of the discourse (and thereby experience) of feminism in opposition to more traditional discourses of gender. In this respect the research process is, potentially at least, empowering.

The process of self-discovery and criticism is another aspect which is possibly empowering. I am aware of criticisms from various quarters that the concentration on self – self-knowledge, self-awareness, flexibility, growth, social skills, which are central to the kind of youth work and group work practice I have a little experience in – is intrinsically reactionary because it is individualistic, and focuses energy at the wrong point. It is structures that must be changed, not individuals. But this line of thought is too quick to reject varieties of self-analysis which are progressive because they disturb an, admittedly reactionary, perception of the self as given, fixed, immutable. Problematising gender – whether by critical analysis of mass-marketed romantic stories for girls; or studying the complexity and ambiguity of identity through critical analysis of competing discourses of class and gender (themselves complex and ambiguous) – undermines sexist definitions of 'girlhood' and 'womanhood'.

It has also been pointed out to me that we cannot take it for granted that self-knowledge is always empowering – it might be damaging.[5] In the case of the lower sixth's discussion of class it may seem that we came perilously close to damage.

I have said that the research fell far short of the ideals of 'action research', or research 'on, for and by' the respondents. It has been argued that action research's costs (in terms of loss of analytic clarity, or theoretical testing) are too high, in any case. I have also mentioned that my own theoretical preoccupations were, quite reasonably, of no interest to the girls. What has happened in this research, though, is that the girls have taken part in a process of constructing themselves as objects, seeing themselves as social actors. In the research process they could look at themselves from the researcher's angle.

It might well be asked (and has been) however, whether empowering these public school girls, by enhancing their understanding of class identity and relations, is really a defensible project. This takes us on to the question of 'standpoints'. I have already pointed out problems with the feminist sociology and epistemology which postulate a shared feminine standpoint. To begin with, it is clear that if we call the orthodox scientific standpoint 'male' then we must commit ourselves to acknowledging that some women have taken up this male standpoint. We might agree that it is typically more difficult for a woman to remain oblivious to the shortcomings of this stance than it is for a man, but we cannot hold that 'women' and the 'feminine standpoint' are coextensive. When we begin to analyse other social structures such as class, race or ethnicity, and so on, the difficulties in the proposition that a woman researching women will share a standpoint with her respondents become more marked.

In this case, it seems to me that to an extent I shared a femininity with the girls – on questions like the double sexual standard, the representations of femininity we have to cope with when reading women's magazines, and so on. On the other hand I could not share the ethnic position of some of the girls in the youth project group, or the class position of the public school girls. Indeed, in the latter case, my position is positively antagonistic to these girls. They might have stones thrown at their horses when they're riding past; but these girls canter back to houses with stables, skiing holidays, designer clothes, jobs as directors' cooks, and, probably, marriages to wealthy men. But here is the point at which I can clarify the merits of doing this kind of work with these girls. The class relations, shot through with ambiguities of acknowledgement and denial, in which these girls move and find themselves, are class relations which involve gender relations of a particular sort. The rules which tell these girls not to flirt at parties, and not to be called 'Sharon' are not, in their experience, separable. Their upper-class identity is only compatible with a subordinate gender identity. In this case, then, to disturb one is to disturb the other.

Now I do not think that the materiality of this sociological relation has been made quite plain to the girls in the course of the research. I have already outlined the limits to the process of 'feeding back' the results – in the end the feeding-back process only constructed more data for me. Further than this, though, these are *sociological* results, couched in the particular language of that discipline. Giving a series of lectures or classes on sociology was not part of the deal, and not what the girls wanted, in this case. Nevertheless, the sociological version of this is not the only one – but participating in sociological research opened up new ways of knowing for the girls.

NOTES

1 The research from the Centre for Contemporary Cultural Studies at Birmingham University (including Griffin 1985, McRobbie 1978, Willis 1980) was most influential.
2 A good example of this analytical and methodological approach is Lees (1986).
3 Perhaps the most famous example is Whyte (1955).
4 For further discussion of 'damage limitation' in the research process, see the section on Ethics in the Introduction.
5 This issue arose in discussions with my co-authors.

5

'RESPECT, PLEASE!': INVESTIGATING RACE, POWER AND LANGUAGE

Deborah Cameron

INTRODUCTION

This chapter gives an account of some work carried out in 1986 with young Afro-Caribbeans in a London youth club. A group of young people, together with two youth workers and a sociolinguist (me) spent some weeks exploring issues of racism, Black history and ethnic identity in relation to language, eventually producing a video on these topics which we entitled 'Respect, Please!'.

In what follows, I will talk about the reasons for undertaking such a project, give an account of our activities and of the video itself, and then try to relate these things to the ideas about research methods discussed in the Introduction of this book. In particular, I will ask in what ways and to what extent the project 'empowered' those who took part.

It should be said at once that the project's aims and implications look clearer and more coherent to me now than they did at the time. In a sense I am imposing a structure I could not have perceived during the project itself. For what the group and I did was not conceived as an exemplary piece of empowering research. It would be more accurate to say that my involvement in this project led me to think in a more self-conscious way about the possibilities of what I, with the other researchers represented in this book, would later come to think of as an 'empowerment' position. This makes my work different from, say, Elizabeth Frazer's in the previous chapter. Frazer had thought much more seriously in advance about how best to ensure that both she and her informants would benefit from the research process; whereas I had very little idea what might come out of this work when I began it.

In fact, the project reported in this chapter differs strikingly from all the other case histories in this book. Unconstrained by any institutional requirements, accountable to no-one except myself and my informants (no supervisor, no funding body, no journal editor or publisher), I was entirely free to work in unconventional (some might say unscholarly)

113

ways, whereas all the other contributors were researching for Ph.Ds, which obliged them to adopt a particular framework and modify or subvert it from within. One consequence of this is that their projects are much more clearly examples of 'research'. In my own discussion I will be concerned to examine a question that the other case histories do not raise, or not to the same extent: what constitutes something as 'research'?

'RESPECT, PLEASE!': AN OUTLINE

The project was carried out at Charterhouse in Southwark, south London, a youth club serving a working-class inner-city area with an ethnically diverse population (though the group I worked with was mainly Afro-Caribbean – members of other ethnic groups sometimes participated in a discussion, but none was involved on a regular basis and none took part in the video – the club's membership, by contrast with many London youth clubs, is explicitly multiracial, and this is significant). Charterhouse provides a range of activities and services, in all of which it cultivates an ethos of anti-racism and anti-sexism, placing emphasis on the development of interpersonal skills (expressing one's own views and responding sensitively to those expressed by others). Many club members have been involved with Charterhouse for a period of years; the Coffee Bar Club, a weekly discussion group for those aged 16+, had a core of regular attenders with highly developed skills and consciousness. It was this group which participated in the 'Respect, Please!' project.

I first went to the club at the invitation of a youth worker, to lead a session on sexism in language. In my initial presentation I made analogies between sexism and racism, on the assumption that racist language would be a more immediately obvious concept for a mainly Black group. It soon became clear that this – racism – was what they wanted to talk about. At their request I agreed to go on meeting them until they felt the topic had been fully explored. After a while, it was suggested we should make some record of our discussions. We began by tape recording, but eventually had the notion of making our talk more widely accessible by producing a short video. Thereafter, we worked to decide what should go into the video and in what form it should be presented. The project ended when the video was completed: with a long and chaotic Saturday session during which we rehearsed, recorded and planned the editing of our text.

During the weeks when we were meeting, our main activity was discussion. We went over the same things again and again, beginning always from the experience of group members. Two main subjects preoccupied us: one was verbal racism, while the other was the linguistic heritage of Afro-Caribbeans in Britain.

The topic of racist language was the first one the group initiated. Individuals recalled incidents of being called 'nigger' in the street, cracks from white workmates about 'suntans', cringeing from words like 'coloured' and 'immigrant', from the unthinking use of expressions like 'black list' or 'black sheep', from the constant enquiries about 'where are you from?' and from language used consciously or unconsciously to divide 'us' from 'them'. We talked about the feelings of anger and pain these insults caused, and discussed the possibility of challenging racist language. We also talked more theoretically about the way languages evolve to reflect and reinforce the structures of the wider society, thus addressing the question of how this vocabulary of racism comes to be available to British English speakers.

The topic of language as it is used by Black British speakers was initiated by me, though the group responded enthusiastically. Again, the starting point was personal experience. People recalled occasions when their parents, knowing their island accents to be a source of embarassment and stigma as well as misunderstanding, had relied on their children to conduct important business on the telephone. They spoke of listening to relatives talking in patois, and in some cases recalled being excluded because their parents felt they would get on better if they spoke only 'proper English'. They talked about the verbal repertoire young Afro-Caribbeans in London have access to and their feelings about it; they talked (a great deal) about differences between people whose families had come from different parts of the Caribbean.

I intervened much more in these discussions than in the discussions of racist language. I told them about the historical formation of creoles under slavery, sketching their relationship to European and African languages. I talked, also, about the sources of prejudice towards working-class and Black speech, and about the arguments of socio-linguists that all varieties are linguistically equal. I did this because it was evident the group had more ambivalent views about the way they, and more especially their parents, talked than they did about the way White people used language against them. They lacked the information and the analysis which they needed to arrive at a clear position on patois. I noticed this with interest, and in due course I must return to it.

The video we made brought the two topics together. The title chosen, 'Respect, Please!' was intended to convey both that the language used by Black people should be respected and that the language used by society in general should show respect for Black people by avoiding racist and ethnocentric expressions.

The video has at its centre two filmed group discussions, one dealing with racist language and the other with attitudes to the speech of Black British people. These discussions mix accounts of personal experience and analysis of what the experience signifies. They are framed in the video by dramatic and comic role-plays in which particular situations familiar to group members are acted out – for example, a Black British woman is asked by a workmate where she 'comes from'. Other scenes are drawn from news reports. Someone had read that the Metropolitan Police had taken lessons in Jamaican creole, the better to understand muggers and dope dealers. This absurd and racist notion was parodied in a 'police academy' scene in which recruits repeat patois expressions after their Jamaican teacher. The final scene of the video is a 'News At Ten' style summary: 'And now the main points again.' The main points are that the conventions of ordinary English usage are racist, that attitudes to Black speech are ignorant and racist, and that 'if the language is right, the colour is wrong' – in other words, if Black Britons give up their linguistic heritage this will not save them from discrimination in face-to-face encounters. The concluding message, delivered this time in patois, is that Black speakers are not 'foreign' but part of British society. They should be proud of their heritage, and others should treat it with respect.

IMPLICATIONS: EMPOWERMENT VERSUS ADVOCACY

It might well be asked at this point whether the project reported above has any wider significance apart from its effect on the particular group of people who worked on it. After all, there is nothing novel about sociolinguists working in Black communities; indeed it could be said that this kind of work is the jewel in the crown of the 'advocacy position'. Not only is a great deal known about Black Englishes, especially in the USA, that knowledge has been used quite explicitly with the intention of benefiting the community (most obviously in Labov's polemic 'The logic of nonstandard English' (1969) and in the Ann Arbor case which we outlined in the Introduction). Knowledge of Afro-Caribbean varieties and of the Black varieties used in Britain has grown more slowly, but in recent years more support has been forthcoming and we are now seeing the results (cf. Dalphinis 1985; Devonish 1986; Edwards 1986; Hewitt 1986; Sutcliffe 1982).

Research on Black speech has added to linguists' knowledge, then, and the knowledge itself has been used in socially responsible ways. Even if we suspect that some of the research may have been funded by the state in the hope of solving embarrassing political problems like the under-achievement of Black schoolchildren without tackling deeply rooted institutional racism, that is not the effect it has usually had. Linguists have refused to locate the problem in language and have pointed instead to ignorance, prejudice and the alienation these engender.

I did not doubt the good intentions, nor the impressive achievements, of these sociolinguists when I began to work at Charterhouse, and I do not doubt them now. The project I took part in made me question, however, how far their not-insignificant accumulation of knowledge and its dissemination to state and other institutions has actually empowered members of the Black community. This question concerns what we might call the social distribution of knowledge, and it is so important in my evaluation of the Charterhouse project that I want to discuss it here in more detail. The wider significance of 'Respect, Please!', I will argue, lies in its attempt to redistribute knowledge about language in Black communities.

The social distribution of knowledge

There are two questions that need to be asked about knowledge. Who is it made by, and who is it made for? In the case of knowledge about the language of Black communities, the answers are as follows: knowledge is made by linguists (who as a group are overwhelmingly white and middle class; even if they are not, they are trained in a socially elite tradition that distances them from the community they study) and it is made for two groups – other linguists, and language professionals like teachers and speech therapists whose interest is practical, because they are likely to have Black clients.

This structure of knowledge has a number of socially significant consequences. First, the definition and the content of knowledge takes on the perspective of the knowers rather than the known, reflecting the priorities of the former group. Thus at Charterhouse, the young people constantly articulated their knowledge of language being used to insult and demean them. They made it clear that this was their first priority in trying to understand the workings of language. Yet in how much academic writing about language in Black communities is this matter so much as mentioned in passing? It is certainly not a priority in the professional literature. And indeed, to the extent that they are outsiders using the distancing strategies of positivist research, linguists are not in a good position to elicit this particular knowledge.

A second consequence of the structure of knowledge referred to above is that the ideas and arguments produced by linguists, their systematised accounts of linguistic structure, variation and history, never get back to the language-using community. This remains a discourse of experts talking to other experts.

It is worth asking why this should matter. It might be said, for instance, that expert linguistic knowledge is too arcane to be of interest to anyone but a professional linguist. The same is true of most professional and expert knowledge, to which ordinary laypeople neither need nor want to have access. Witness the fact that if I get into a mess with my finances, I do not go to the trouble of learning a body of relevant knowledge, I simply employ an accountant to do it for me. So long as the accountant's services are available to all, there is surely nothing wrong with knowledge remaining in her hands, inaccessible to me. Similarly, if linguists are prepared to act as advocates for the community, the community does not need to have access to their knowledge.

Yet I do not think that knowing about your language can be justly compared to knowing about double-entry bookkeeping. Knowledge about your language is knowledge about yourself and your history. The force of that only struck me after I had spent several weeks talking to the young people at Charterhouse. Early on I had discovered that most of them shared a common perception of Caribbean creoles as 'broken language' – a view transmitted not only by the wider culture but more specifically by their parents, who in some cases took steps to prevent them learning their ancestral patois. Not one person in the group knew anything about the origins of pidgin and creole languages under slavery; not one person had ever heard that Caribbean creoles have African antecedents. (Compare this to what just about every schoolchild knows about the relation of standard English and Latin.) When I explained these things, it made an immediate and dramatic difference to the group's way of talking about their own and their parents' speech. They insisted (overruling me) on putting into the video a completely 'straight' mini-lecture on the definition of a creole and its claim to be an autonomous language. And some of them were clearly angry that this knowledge, so casually deployed by a white linguist, had been denied to them. They believed the denial was deliberate, and they related it to the more general absence of Black history and culture from the school curriculum.

More than anything else, this unexpectedly strong reaction convinced me that for sociolinguists to practise advocacy, while clearly necessary is far from sufficient. It is not enough that linguists and teachers and speech therapists should know about Black varieties and accept their structural complexity, communicative adequacy and so on. Black speakers themselves should possess the relevant information and the analytic tools to make use of it in ways which they determine. In cases like the Ann Arbor trial (see p. 15) it is doubtless appropriate for linguist-advocates to take the stand as expert witnesses. But people also need ammunition for use in the struggles of their daily lives.

We can sum up the consequences of an unequal distribution of knowledge like this. Some kinds of knowledge, grounded in experience, tend to remain in the community and are not expressed in academic discourse (the prevalence and significance of racist verbal abuse is an example. I certainly could not, before going to Charterhouse, have begun to guess the frequency with which any single Black person encounters racist abuse; now I think of it as a major social problem, quite unjustifiably ignored.). Other kinds of knowledge remain the province of the 'experts' and do not get back to the community. The net effect is disadvantageous to the community. On the one hand, its experience and its priorities are marginalised, while on the other it is denied knowledge that would be interesting and useful to it. The Charterhouse project was about redistributing knowledge so that the community could say what it knew to a wider audience and at the same time gain access to what linguists know. I believe this kind of exchange to be an important dimension of interactive and empowering research.

THE PROJECT AS EMPOWERING RESEARCH: SOME CONSIDERATIONS

I have already observed that the project was not conceived as an exemplar of empowering research, or indeed as research at all. Initially I was simply responding to a youth worker's request that I lead a session. Nevertheless it will be clear by now that I believe the work that resulted to have been research and to have been, to some degree at least, empowering. Here I want to consider, in relation to the project, some of the methodological questions we raised in the Introduction. What ways of approaching issues of racism and language contributed to the success of the project, and how might they have been improved? How do the methods used in Southwark relate to the programmatic statements we have made (see pp. 23–6) about interacting with subjects, respecting their agendas and sharing knowledge with them?

Agenda setting

In the Introduction we raised the possibility of designing research to meet the needs of both researcher and researched. Initially, I did not regard myself as a researcher in this context, and I conceived what I was doing to be responding to the group's interest in a particular topic. In other words, there was no agenda as such. But that changed with the decision to make a video. To justify the commitment and the effort involved, it was necessary for all of us to define a mutually agreeable agenda and so design a project that would meet their needs and mine.

The group's main concern was to make the issues we had been discussing accessible to a wider audience. They wanted the video to be usable in other youth clubs and discussion groups which would then be able to to address questions of language and racism in a more structured and informed way. The audiences they had in mind were both Black people – for whom the video would function as a validation of experience and an analysis of that experience – and white people, for whom it would provide a way into something they might not have thought about, even if they were in principle anti-racist. For example, it was suggested that the video might be shown to the trustees of the club. I know that one of the women involved later showed 'Respect, Please!' at her nursery nursing course.

Here, a criticism should be made. When the project was over, there was no 'follow up' from me; to all intents and purposes I disappeared from the group. That does not mean the project had no long-term effects, but rather that I made no effort to check or document these. Obviously a question is raised here about the researcher's ongoing responsibility in research done within the 'empowerment' framework.

My own agenda had been different from the group's. As a lecturer in linguistics, I teach mainly white students, but linguistic diversity and racism in language are subjects I address with them. I wanted something I could use as a teaching aid to get the points I thought important across. It was crucial to me to have materials in which Black people would speak rather than just be spoken about by me. But there were nevertheless things which I wanted the group to address for the benefit of my students. In the event, I found the video useful for teaching. Its most obvious merit is to provide direct personal testimony about racism: this discourages the sort of abstract discussion white students are apt to take refuge in, and prevents the issue being trivialised.

I think that the group, like me, would be in strong agreement with Penelope Harvey (chapter 3) when she argues that 'empowering research must be directed as much at the political consciousness of the powerful as of the powerless' (p. 88). The agendas just outlined show it was important to us all to produce a powerful, anti-stereotypical representation of certain linguistic practices and concerns in the hope of altering not only the group's own perceptions – though this did happen on the question of patois – but also the perceptions of people outside the group. As Harvey says, to do this can be empowering in the sense that it affects future interactions with outsiders and decisions outsiders might make. I would add to her observation that even to *imagine yourself doing it* can be empowering. The group's pleasure in the idea of the video, the idea that someone else (my students, for example) might attend to what they were saying, was evident.

In the course of the project I discovered an additional agenda, which was to learn something about the sociolinguistics of this particular Black community. The structure of Black Englishes is by no means a primary research interest of mine, and I would not claim expertise in this field. But the issues that came up in the group touch on more general questions of language, identity and power, questions which are close to my interests and which I will discuss in a later section.

Process and product

Since it is interactive – a point we argued at length in the introductory chapter of this book – empowering research must give attention to the research process as well as the research product. In this case, rather untypically, the product (the video itself) was fully accessible to those who made it (consider the difference in accessibility if I had written a report on the project instead). Even so, the process of discussion and analysis was an important part of what we achieved. Indeed I would say that the changes brought about in our attitudes and perceptions through concentrated thinking and talking were more significant, and probably longer-lived, than the video.

Because we were working in a safe setting and over an indefinite period, it was possible for discussions to be very intense. Often they were frankly emotional. They were also repetitious: in another research context, with limited time or more formal interactions, it would not have been possible just to let things go on so that the same experiences were retold over and over. Indeed, when this happened I often caught myself wondering if we were 'getting anywhere'. In retrospect, however, I think it is an important consideration for empowering research that people should be able to approach a topic in their own way and at their own pace. A focus on personal narratives may also help to reduce the inequality between expert researcher and researched.

In this particular case, the nature of the product also helped to stress the group's expertise as opposed to mine. A video is inherently a co-operative enterprise for which a range of different skills is needed. The group had made videos before and had developed the relevant skills – such as dramatic improvisation – to a high level. The video makes abundantly clear that they are competent, more competent than I. And once again, the need for co-operative work generated more discussion, more 'process'.

Sharing knowledge

In the Introduction we addressed the idea that there is merit in sharing research results with informants, and more generally, expert knowledge. In this project, there were no results as such – rather, the group's experiential knowledge was shared with me. But my sharing expert knowledge played an important part in the overall project.

It was not particularly difficult to share with the group what I know about the history and nature of Caribbean creoles, despite the fact that I am not a specialist in that field. But when it came to my telling them what linguists who are specialists have written about the development of British Black English, things were slightly different. They did not accept

121

all the prevailing wisdom on this subject and they were quick to challenge me.

For example, the literature (e.g. Sutcliffe 1982) holds that many younger Black speakers in Britain, and especially in London, use a variety that can reasonably be described as 'Jamaican'. This functions as a general marker of young people's Black identity, even when they are descended from people who came from other parts of the Caribbean. The Charterhouse group was interesting in that the families of its members had come from a range of geographical areas, and it contained few speakers of Jamaican descent. The group strongly rejected the idea that inter-island differences had been levelled among their peer groups. They spoke knowledgeably about such differences, making it clear that terms like 'Bajan' and 'St Lucian' have a social significance and a demonstrable linguistic content to them. In the case of St Lucian (also Dominican) there is the further point that this is a French rather than an English creole. Suspicion and antagonism between English and French patois speakers was discussed often and in detail by the Charterhouse group. The common perception of Jamaican as the unmarked Caribbean language and culture in Britain was denied and indeed resented.

What this shows is not that the existing literature is wrong but that Black British speakers are not uniform in their attitudes and behaviour. Different types of Black community exist and indeed are in a state of change. Doubtless those researchers who have worked in Black communities in Britain would agree that the question of identity among young Black British speakers would support more empirical research. This brings me to the last issue I want to discuss, namely what I as a linguist gained from participating in this project and conducting it in this way.

EMPOWERING RESEARCH AS RESEARCH: WHAT LINGUISTS CAN LEARN

I have already said more than once that when we embarked on the 'Respect, Please!' project I did not really regard it as a piece of research. I regarded it, essentially, as youth work; secondarily I saw in it a way of getting useful teaching materials. Unlike the other contributors to this book, I was in no way constrained by the institutional structures we associate with research projects: I was not called upon to report to a funding body, produce a thesis or indeed publish my findings. It is not surprising, therefore, that the question most often put to me about 'Respect, Please!' is whether it really *was* a piece of research.

This is a surprisingly difficult question. Participating in the project problematised the whole category of 'research' for me. Who decides what counts as research, and on what criteria do they base the decision?

It seems to me that most academics operate with what we may call the 'Ph.D.' definition. Research is that which makes an original contribution to the field, and the judgement of whether something is original and within the field rests with a jury of one's peers, i.e. other academics in the same discipline whose own credentials have been validated in the same way. To enter the charmed circle of expertise you have to satisfy someone already in it that you have carried out something they would recognise as research. It is usually assumed, too, that 'real' research is worthy of publication; the knowledge it brings forth will enter the public domain (though it seems to me worth noting that this so-called public domain can be very limited – academic journals and books are accessible only to a privileged few – and also that the requirement to 'go public' is quite frequently waived. Many *bona fide* research programmes do not publish their results for commercial or political reasons.).

Research is also defined by what it is not. Thus teaching is not research, nor is writing a textbook. Consultancy – the giving of expert advice to a business or community group or political party – is not research.

The trouble is, these are definitions promulgated and sustained by the authority of particular institutions, and I am not sure how far a politically responsible seeker of knowledge should agree to respect them. For example, how far is it helpful or even feasible to make a distinction between teaching and research, or community work and research? In my experience, the boundaries are very often much fuzzier than the Ph.D. definition would suggest. Harvey's account of her experiences in the field (chapter 3) echoes a body of ethnographic work suggesting that the lived reality of field research is very complex, the division of activities into 'research' and 'not-research' futile or impossible.

Furthermore, we must consider what interests the division serves. At present in Britain the distinction between teaching and research is being used by educational policy-makers to reinforce professional hierarchies in higher education institutions. The favoured few who do research and publish will be rewarded with money and status, while those who just teach will be downgraded. There is also good reason to worry about the 'gatekeeping' function of a narrow definition. If a few acknowledged authorities define 'research', they also decide what kinds of knowledge will be allowed to enter the public domain; by giving or withholding funding, by refereeing for journals and publishers, by steering graduate students in one direction rather than another, these people can essentially set the discipline's agenda, pronouncing certain topics, methodologies and conclusions legitimate while others are off-limits.

Recently, for instance, I received an announcement of a new journal in sociolinguistics, which explicitly stated its commitment to research using sophisticated statistical methods. No-one who has doubts about a particular version of the quantitative paradigm or who wishes to employ 'holistic' (let alone 'empowering') techniques, can expect to publish their work in this journal. Another somewhat different instance that comes to mind is the long neglect of pidgin and creole languages, which linguists were warned off for years (Muehlhausler 1986). Obviously, these gatekeeping practices are difficult to challenge, let alone eliminate. But I am trying to suggest that the category of research – like the canons of knowledge in general – is by no means a transparent one. It is highly constructed, often authoritarian, and has a hidden political agenda.

All in all, I would prefer a broad definition of research, one that recognises it can be done by people other than professional academics and for different types of audience – if a few hundred academic colleagues scattered over the globe count as the public domain, why not a few dozen people in a particular local community? Any active involvement in finding out something you did not know before must have a claim to the title 'research'. That some instances may prove more valuable, more influential and more lasting than others I do not dispute. But I would want to insist that a project is not devoid of value because its impact is limited to a narrowly circumscribed time and place. In the long run, that is the fate of most of what we unquestioningly accept as research – a point to which the pile of unread Ph.D. theses in every university library bears eloquent, silent witness.

The Charterhouse project, which I initially regarded as a teaching/youth work exercise, did in fact generate new knowledge for me as well as for the group. It suggested new questions to me and threw light on questions I was already familiar with. It is of course true that had I foreseen this I might have designed the project's activities differently. I might have been more systematic about what was discussed from week to week, I might have reviewed the literature more thoroughly, followed up better, and so on. I think now that the project had more research potential than I chose to exploit. But even in prioritising the 'not-research' aspects of the project I found out enough to prompt a certain rethinking of my ideas, which came in the main from published literature on Black British speech.

The project raised questions I had not previously thought to ask. For example, what are the functions of bidialectalism among young Black British speakers? I had conceived of their competence in both patois and non-standard localised varieties primarily in the terms of what sociolinguists call 'acts of identity', that is, an extensive verbal repertoire is used to mark allegiance to particular groups and values in particular contexts. Although this appears to be true for the Charterhouse group it is not the whole story. Young women in particular made a number of interesting comments about the way their parents and older relations used them as interpreters in encounters with 'the authorities'.

JOANNE: Yeah coz my parents, well my mum, if there's any important phone calls to be made (...) then she'll always say oh you phone, they'll understand you.

SHERYL: Because thing is, people keep putting down the way they speak, they've got such heavy accents that they are afraid to speak to anyone in authority, like school and that, they want you to come with them, they can speak through you, which I think is a bit sad really.

JOANNE: (...) I wish they would talk how they are, be what they are.

The ability of these young women to speak a more socially acceptable English had been crucial to their families' institutional negotiations. It was evident that the young women themselves had ambivalent feelings about their role as 'mediators' (a role often assigned to young minority women; cf. Zentella 1987 on the New York Puerto Rican community). They sometimes expressed resentment of the extra responsibility placed upon them while at other times they spoke of the distress they felt on their mothers' behalf in particular. I was interested in this because although the issue of mediation has been discussed as it concerns bilinguals, as far as I know it has not been raised in relation to British Afro-Caribbeans.

A second example which illustrates how the project raised new questions for me as a linguist is that of inter-island differences and how far they remain important to a British-born generation. At the level of discourse or attitude, and to some extent behaviour, these differences clearly had considerable importance for the Charterhouse group. How was I to account for their apparent difference from the informants in standard published studies? (Of course, Edwards (1986) studied informants who were themselves of Jamaican descent, whereas only one or two of my subjects fell into that category. But it is a general point in studies of Black British English that inter-island differences have lost much of their significance.)

When I have discussed this question with other linguists, it has been suggested to me that there is a simple explanation: mine was a totally unrepresentative sample. In fact, they were what Labov would call 'lames', either isolated from or peripheral to the Black subcultures that exist in London. These young people had consciously chosen to attend a multiracial youth club (whereas it would be possible, in Southwark, to find clubs where the membership is self-consciously Black); and most were employed. Their social networks were therefore less 'Black' than those of many Afro-Caribbeans in London. Significantly, the video shows them consistently claiming the identity 'Black British' as opposed to other available labels (such as Black, Afro-Caribbean, Bajan, St Lucian, African, etc.). There is obviously a political shading to these self-attributions, and it is one of which group members were well aware.

It seems to me this raises a general issue for sociolinguistics. As Ben Rampton (chapter 2) also notes, group membership and self-perception are complex matters: the 'member' versus 'lame' opposition Labov articulated in his work on Harlem adolescent peer groups is over-simple, and tends to mythologise the figure of the 'real' vernacular user (who is often personified as young, male and Black). Viv Edwards (1989) has discussed the implications of this mythology in relation to the treatment of minority *women* in sociolinguistic studies; she argues that it has been distorting, causing us to lose sight of interesting patterns.

However, because of its emphasis on overcoming the observer's paradox and getting to the vernacular, sociolinguistics has often been unable to make use of people's own rich understanding of the complexity of identity. Attitudinal data have often been either superficial or artificially constrained by the positivist techniques of, for instance, matched guise testing. In the research at Charterhouse, where I was obliged to pursue interactive methods and be completely open about my purposes, it was much easier to engage in detailed discussion of attitudes to language. What I lost on the swings of unselfconscious linguistic performance, I gained, precisely, on the roundabouts of making people reflect consciously on the point at issue. In my view, this was a real gain, and shows that empowering research does not have to be invalid or uninteresting.

I would also want to argue that sociolinguists will make more effective advocates if they know how the community itself perceives the matter in hand. For example, the constant linking of attitudes to Caribbean language with racist verbal abuse is indicative of a perspective in which racism rather than just 'race' is the starting point and primary reality. This needs to be understood by any sensitive advocate (as I think it was in Ann Arbor). I was struck by the fact that when we discussed insults we concerned ourselves as much with white speech as with Black. Referring to a range of expressions used at her workplace, such as 'Black bastards', 'working like niggers', 'the natives are restless', etc., one young woman said, to general agreement, 'To them [i.e. white people] it's just everyday talk, innit?' I was being reminded here that to take Black speech as the normal object of concern – the problem, in fact – is not good enough. From a Black perspective the problem lies in the unremarked everyday racism of white discourse, and it is only right this be analysed too.

This is one of the things that is meant by 'redefining knowledge', i.e. rethinking what counts as knowledge and what phenomena need to be

126

known about, as well as redistributing knowledge. It relates to what feminists have called 'standpoint epistemology'. The idea behind this is that reality looks different from the perspective of the dominant and that of the subordinated; and there might be a reason to privilege the understanding of a subordinate group as 'a morally and scientifically preferable grounding for our interpretations and explanations of nature and social life' (Harding 1986: 26). Presumably the subordinated have no interest in maintaining what Harding calls 'partial and perverse' understandings whose hidden agenda is the maintenance of domination. At the same time, their own understandings are enriched by actual experience.

There are, of course, criticisms to be made of standpoint epistemology, and not only the predictable objections of positivists that it is biased. We must be wary of the notion that there is one Black or feminist standpoint: women and people of colour are not homogeneous groups, except from the discreditable perspective of their sexist and racist oppressors. More radically, postmodernist feminists would want to cast doubt on the possibility of any 'correct', or even 'more correct' account of reality: as Jane Flax (1986: 17) observes, 'Perhaps "reality" can have "a" structure only from the falsely universalising perspective of the master.'

That said, I think that some kind of standpoint epistemology that privileges insider knowledge is useful to the project of empowering research. There is a similarity here with the ethnographer's concern not to filter informants' ways of seeing through a mesh of western preconceptions; and with the feminist principle of 'starting where people are'. For the expert researcher to entertain the notion that her informants are in some sense 'right' is, I think, an enabling strategy which at least sets up a productive dialogue with the researched as full participants.

This is not to say that the 'insider' interpretation will end up dominating. In the Charterhouse case I did not think the group was 'right' in their view of patois as 'broken language': I tried to challenge that interpretation and I think I succeeded. Conversely, though, I was prepared to take on challenges to my own ways of thinking; to reconceive these as irrelevant or misguided or reflections of particular academic interests rather than some higher 'truth'.

CONCLUSION: SOME POINTS ABOUT RESEARCHER AND RESEARCHED

As a white linguist I had always felt uneasy about the idea of doing research in Black communities. I read the work of colleagues like David Sutcliffe and Viv Edwards with respect, I agreed it was useful and interesting to have the information their research provided, but I would not have chosen to go into their field. I suspect that many white linguists, including some who are experts on Black Englishes, feel the same way; certainly they greet the entry of Black linguists to the field with pleasure and relief. The crucial role of such linguists in the Ann Arbor case (and indeed the pioneering work of older Black scholars whose merits were not always widely recognised) is routinely acknowledged.

It may be true that linguists who come from a community are better placed to work with that community's language; it is certainly desirable that the academic community should draw from a wider social and ethnic base. But the real problem, I now believe, is the division between researcher and researched itself. The only way to deal with the ethical problems that are posed by research with subordinated groups (and in linguistics, though Black speakers have been the classic example they are by no means the only one) is to give those groups more control over what is done in research and how.

After I stopped working at Charterhouse I formulated a number of guidelines for my own future work. They were as follows:

1 Ask questions that interest the researched group or are generated by them.
2 Be open about your agenda and negotiate at all stages.
3 Make the knowledge and perceptions of the researched group count; do not impose an 'expert' framework unthinkingly.
4 On the other hand, share information and analytic tools; the group may reject them but it is wrong to assume from the outset they do not want to know.
5 Present what you learn from research in such a way that the researched group will find it accessible.

Some of these (e.g. 1, 5) are ideals that may not be realisable; others (e.g. 2) are fundamental. None, of course, should be taken as totally novel within sociolinguistics, for on the contrary each has been observed as a matter of good practice rather than explicitly formulated policy by at least some sociolinguists since the mid-1960s.

It is also important to note that I am not trying to place the interests of the researched above those of the researcher (who in most cases will be more constrained than I was in Southwark). Rather I am proposing that we should seek to ensure compatibility of interests as far as possible; and that sociolinguistic analysis should be more widely available, right to the grass roots.

I feel most strongly about this second point. If sociolinguistics has an axiomatic, programmatic statement to proclaim to the world, it is surely the doctrine of 'linguistic equality', i.e. that all varieties are equal in terms of potential complexity and communicative resources, and that assertions to the contrary rest on no linguistic foundation, but rather on social prejudice (for a discussion of what is and is not entailed by the equality claim, see Hudson 1983). The political implications of this are far reaching, as sociolinguists and their conservative opponents have not been slow to perceive.

Yet the community I worked in had never remotely heard of the axiom. No educated parent or enlightened teacher had ever shared it with them. I acknowledge, of course, that in some schools language-awareness materials are now used to get the point across: some of the activities they contain are similar to ones I used at Charterhouse. I am bound to say, though, that the group I worked with had never come across anything like them before. Nor do I believe that schooling is the only or the best medium through which knowledge can or should be disseminated to people in the community (see Cameron 1989).

It is important that linguists do not over-simplify the doctrine of linguistic equality (see also Rampton's discussion in chapter 2), and that they refrain from attempting to pre-determine the outcome of any debate on it within communities they do not belong to. Some of the more extreme and glib defences of nonstandard varieties by well-intentioned linguists have been counterproductive and divisive, since people can see perfectly well that all varieties are not equal, and wonder what world linguists live in. Perhaps some professionals have been guilty of ignoring the principle, 'start where people are', and reluctant to permit them to arrive at their own positions.

For instance, it is evident that the consensus about American Vernacular Black English celebrated in Labov's paper on the Ann Arbor case (1982) does not extend as far as we might think if we read only that one paper. Some of Labov's most bitter opponents have been Afro-American intellectuals who believe the effect of his work will be further to disadvantage inner-city children – a sort of John Honeyesque, 'language trap' argument, but in this instance, rather awkwardly, coming from Black scholars with radical credentials. Then again, there are radicals who feel that in establishing the right of the Ann Arbor children to special provision *for the learning of standard English* sociolinguists involved in the case did not go far enough.

Where this sort of disagreement arises it is not for the 'expert' to close it down: rather it is her responsibility where possible to respect the wishes of the community (as happened in Ann Arbor; the parents undoubtedly wanted their children to learn standard English), and where this is not possible, because the community itself is divided, to encourage and facilitate open, informed debate. At the point of political action, a linguist's opinion is, at best, no better than anyone else's. When you make available knowledge in the hope of contributing to empowerment, you cannot expect to retain full control of the way it is used. The community must make of knowledge what it will.

Sociolinguists have long understood how language is implicated in social inferiority, both ascribed from the outside and felt from within. It is only when those who actually experience this appropriate expert understandings and act on such understandings on their own behalf that fundamental change, either at the level of self-perception or of institutional practice, will be possible. The 'Respect, Please!' project was an attempt to make change – on a small scale, for a few people – imaginable and possible.

6

CONCLUSION

In the light of the four case studies, we can begin this conclusion by briefly noting what this book has tried to do. Different kinds of involvement with informants have been outlined – 'on'; 'on and for'; 'on, for and with'. The concepts of ethical, advocate and empowering research positions have been introduced. We have discussed epistemological positions – positivism, relativism, realism – according to the potential which they offer for empowering research and we have generally opted for realism. We have emphasised the importance of the non-unified subject for the discussion of researcher–researched relations: not only are the *researched* non-unified subjects, but researchers are too, their identities partly negotiated in the field as well as brought into it. We have scrutinised particular methods (such as participant observation, covert recording and interviews), and have discussed the methodologies of specific research programmes, identifying those which do and those which do not permit empowerment (cf. Rampton on variationist sociolinguistics and the ethnography of communication, Harvey on anthropological field methods, and Frazer on developments within feminist social science). We have identified the importance of political criteria above and beyond method which influence the potential for empowerment, such as the kinds of institutional involvement which made particular projects possible. Is it now any clearer what empowering research requires?

We ended the Introduction with three programmatic statements, precepts with which one might try to guide empowering research. Their formulation was fairly bold: 'Persons are not objects and should not be treated as objects'; 'Subjects have their own agendas and research should try to address them'; 'If knowledge is worth having, it is worth sharing'. In this conclusion it is worth scrutinising these precepts more critically, drawing on the accounts offered in the case studies.

PRECEPT 1: INTERACTIVE METHODS

The assertion that 'People are not objects and should not be treated as objects' is fundamental in any effort to produce empowering research, since it foregrounds the nature of the interaction between researcher and researched in a variety of ways. In this section we focus on methods of data collection, but the issues of interactivity are important during the formulation of research objectives as well as during writing up. We will give more emphasis to these other aspects in subsequent sections when we discuss 'subjects' agendas', 'feedback' and 'other principles'.

Interactive methods entail a dialogue between the researcher and informants which itself then becomes a large part of the data base. They can be contrasted with 'objective' methods where interference in the talk of the researched is discouraged on epistemological grounds. This positivist position seems philosophically naïve, and the case studies suggested that interaction can not only generate opportunities for informants to become more actively involved in the research process, commenting upon and consciously influencing the researcher: interaction can also enhance its eventual findings. Indeed in Cameron's account, the process of sharing linguistic knowledge and experience generated research potential where none had been originally anticipated.

Of course, not all the case studies relied exclusively on dialogue between researcher and informants as a means of data collection. Rampton (chapter 2) used radio microphones to record the playground talk of his informants, and Harvey (chapter 3) recorded the drunken speech of her subjects clandestinely. How far are these methods consistent with criticism of the positivist view that the 'researcher effect' is a deplorable interference? And what of ethical scruples about covert methods? In response to the first question, one can say that covert recording simply produces a different kind of data, interesting for that reason but not intrinsically superior to utterances produced in researcher–informant dialogue.

The second question requires a more complex response, and in formulating this, it is essential first to recognise that this ethical problem is not one that can be confined to the practical level of research method. It inheres in the research relationship itself, rather than in any particular method that a researcher might choose, and it has to be seen as part of the problem of representation. However the data is collected and however negotiated the agendas may have been, when the researcher produces representations of the research for an outside audience, control of the data and its meanings shift very much towards the researcher. She may very well wish to infer implicit meanings in the utterances of informants, even though at the time, the original speaker felt fully conscious of what they were saying and why. Research inevitably involves the recontextualisation of utterances and so even the most deliberate discourses are likely to be reinterpreted. So the line between what is overt and what is covert is much more difficult to draw than the objection to clandestine recording implies. Of course that only complicates the issue: it does not resolve it. We will address questions of representation in a later section.

PRECEPT 2: SUBJECTS' AGENDAS

In formulating the second of our precepts, 'Subjects have their own agendas and research should try to address them', we were concerned (as others have been) to bridge the gap between the preoccupations of informants and those of the researcher. The concerns of researchers are often, and with good reason, quite esoteric. But this need not reduce informants merely to servicing the research.

How was space created for informant agendas in the case studies? From the outset in Cameron's work in Charterhouse (chapter 5), the subject group played a leading role in setting the agenda, and this led to the making of a video, both a process and a product which had value for the group independent of their relationship with the researcher. Neither Rampton (chapter 2), nor Harvey (chapter 3) took their informants' agendas on board in the same way. In Harvey's case this is certainly related to the open-ended nature of her agenda. However, one might also try to explain the difference by claiming that, in contrast to Cameron, both Harvey and Rampton were working towards Ph.D. degrees and were therefore under some pressure to prioritise strictly academic requirements. But then, so too was Frazer: she resolved this by deliberately developing within her project two intersecting but nevertheless distinguishable tracks, one which concentrated on the requirements of a Ph.D. and the other which gave primacy to interests of her subjects. In this way, alongside her own partially independent investigative objectives, she created space within fieldwork for the production of a photo-story, in which traditions in youth work were more influential than traditions in sociology.

With hindsight we would want to suggest that it is not always possible to accommodate informant agendas. The idea itself seems to presuppose that any group of respondents will participate in research already 'knowing itself' in an explicit way and having its own pre-formulated agenda. Nor will such agendas necessarily emerge during the course of the research, and those that do may reflect heterogeneous interests among the group rather than indicating a clear consensus. But if the respondents cannot be fully articulate about their wishes in this respect, we do not want to recommend that the researcher should attempt to formulate their agenda for them (as opposed to facilitating their own attempts to formulate it).

There may also be structural reasons why a researcher is not competent to address the agendas of informants. Category membership is important here, and more particularly the similarities and differences between the social positioning of the researcher and of the researched. Where researcher and researched share some aspect of their social identity, as in chapter 4 where Frazer and her subjects could relate to one another as females in English society, then in a political sense they could be said to share an agenda – especially since gender identity for Frazer was the foreground of her research, not just part of some shared common ground. But elsewhere the researcher can be 'outside' one, some or all of the categories which she has identified as salient for the research, and the experience of a supposedly 'shared' political context can differ according to position and biography (different ethnic groups for instance have radically different experiences of their citizenship).

Lastly, there are likely to be cases where informants do have an agenda, but reject the possibility of help from the researcher. Informants may very clearly percieve what their own interests are, while considering also that the researcher who is sincerely concerned about those interests is nevertheless herself powerless to address them in appropriate ways. A researcher who is in some ways seen as a child, as Harvey was in Ocongate, cannot be expected to help solve adult problems. Children don't empower adults.

PRECEPT 3: FEEDBACK

Our third precept concerned the sharing of knowledge: 'If knowledge is worth having, it is worth sharing.' This is relevant to the findings of the research itself and to sharing academic knowledge more generally – for example, Cameron's point in chapter 5 that she was much better informed about the history of creoles than the subjects themselves. As Cameron also found, though, any social relation in which an expert tells a group about itself is interactionally hazardous. The assymetry involved may require sensitive handling. The role of expert, or teacher, neutralises the hazard to some extent, but no researcher concerned about the power relations between researcher and researched can rely on role alone to manage the difficulty.

The process of feedback can be more or less formalised. The most formal way of meeting the feedback requirement is to convene meetings for the specific purpose of conveying information to the researched (though perhaps with other explicit purposes too). Some institutions – for instance, schools and youth clubs – incorporate expectations that this will be done. Rampton (chapter 2) includes the clearest example of this kind of formal feedback. Harvey (chapter 3) has the most informal approach. Formal feedback is perhaps the most 'honest' because of its greater explicitness. But informal feedback i.e. taking advantage of *ad hoc* opportunities in the field by answering informant questions as they arise, has its advantages too. Given the fluid and more open-ended nature of anthropological participant observation methods, it is not surprising that 'feedback' in these conditions is much more informal and much harder to separate from the collection and analysis of the data.

Not all knowledge is sharable – the researcher's concerns are often quite esoteric. Yet this does not mean that 'empowering' researchers should limit their aims to the pursuit of knowledge which is sharable. This raises questions about the demarcation of research from teaching or community action and about the independent value of research. We will return to these shortly.

One additional kind of knowledge which can usefully be shared is knowledge about the procedures of research – the procedures through which academic knowledge is constructed. This is clearly a valuable enterprise where it can be employed, not because it will turn informants into researchers, but because it will help in the demystification of academic knowledge. Chapter 4, more than any of the others, points in this direction.

OTHER PRINCIPLES

We are conscious, now, of some omissions in our initial account. Two matters in particular deserve further comment. One is the question of representation and its control. The other concerns the broader context in which research is applied – for instance, policy-making.

The power to represent is an important one. During the process of writing up, the social identities of researcher and researched lose part of the fluidity they had during fieldwork, and move towards much greater fixity. One reason for advocating interactive methods lies in the opportunities they provide for participants actively to redefine themselves. Is this negated at the moment of textual representation, when it is the researcher who inevitably takes up a dominating role in selecting and mediating the talk of her subjects?

Feedback can have a role to play here. Rampton (chapter 2), consciously sought 'informed consent' for his representations. For him, the movement to monologic, textual representation for an academic readership was routed through further dialogue with his informants about his findings.

We also have to recognise that empowerment within the micro-context of the research process may entail different considerations from empowerment at the macro-level. To represent informants effectively within the academic frame, so as to influence future research and policy, the voice of the researcher is conventionally privileged. But even where researchers do seek to exert influence 'on behalf of' research subjects and the groups they belong to, researcher-advocacy is not the only option. Potentially useful research findings could be made available to subjects in a form which they themselves can understand – then any advocacy can be instigated by them.

We should now turn more directly to the relation between research and policy, or, more broadly, to the question of the institutional context of research. Although this is an important area, we have had little to say about it. Our own projects have been small-scale and individual. Larger-scale research would have been much more likely to raise a number of fundamental questions about control, funding and application.

Larger-scale research requires greater resources. It is often research commissioned by institutions who are the paymasters of the project. Where there are agendas to be set, those paymasters may feel they have some right to an influence here. Indeed they may have commissioned research with their own interests specifically in mind. Of course, research sponsorship is not intrinsically malign – a researcher who feels compromised in accepting Ministry of Defence money may not feel so if the money comes from the National Health Service.

Some research involves field relations which considerably complicate attempts to be fully open about research agendas. This is especially true with 'triangular' field relations (i.e. those involving researchers, professionals and 'clients', e.g. researchers, youth workers, youth group members; researchers, health workers, patients; researchers, teachers, pupils, and so on). Triangular field relations can be difficult for would-be empowering research, for the desire to empower the client group can involve tensions between researchers and professionals where the latter become conscious that their professional conduct is under critical scrutiny. In other cases, research can be in the public eye not just when it is published, but also when it is in process. Researchers who feel the pressure of this spotlight are often forced to devote a lot of attention to conclusions formulated in advance by people with little sympathy or understanding of the work.

There is also the question of the after-life of research products and the relation of the researcher and researched to that after-life. This has three aspects – local, academic and public. There is a 'local' after-life, of products such as the videotape and the photo-magazine (see chapters 4 and 5), within the community where the products were instigated. It is desirable that academic research should generate such products, and desirable too that they should remain within the control of the researched. There is an academic after-life, of the scholarly articles and books, in so far as they have effects upon the current debates within particular fields of study. And there is after-life in the broader public sphere, where public knowledge and attitudes are shaped, and where policy is formed. Here the researcher can follow the researched into relative powerlessness – losing control of where and how the ideas are disseminated. Obviously, researchers need to think about the potential public uptake of their work, and before committing themselves to a programme of research which might reinforce popular (or scholarly) prejudices and misapprehensions.

THE VALUE OF RESEARCH

In this section we want to account for why it is that we are not arguing for the abandonment of 'research'. Some of our arguments have pointed in that direction. Yet each case study shows we have all presented our activities in terms of their contribution to *research*. The value of research, as an activity distinct from education, and distinct from community action, should be emphasised.

On the one hand, we want to be as clear as we can about what it is we reject in certain traditional notions of what research is, and how this relates to our endorsement of realist over positivist epistemology. On the other hand, we should (if we can) put something in the place of the rejected notions, for we do not want to leave ourselves open to the misinterpretation that we are working with a conception of research so loose as to be vacuous, one in which anything is research that we choose to describe so.

It is important that research continues to be a distinct activity for political reasons. That is, it is politically important to protect a space for the pursuit of knowledge as a valued human enterprise – even if we cannot, in pushing this claim, fall back on the simplistic and misguided argument that the pursuit of knowledge is valuable in so far as it is 'disinterested'. It is also important that the criteria by which research is to be identified should be explicit, for if they are not, then we are dealing with a kind of knowledge which only insiders can really understand, and even their understanding is only tacit.

It is possible to define research in terms of the fairly obvious institutional criteria which it has to satisfy. These are the criteria which Cameron has discussed above (chapter 5): a piece of work is research if it gets a Ph.D., gets published in academic journals, is part of a body of knowledge judged to be authoritative, is valued by accredited academics. There is room for scepticism about the value of some of the work that historically has satisfied these criteria. But that scepticism lacks bite in the absence of an alternative set of criteria that relates to what research *should* be like, to *deserve* accreditation within institutional frameworks.

What, then, do we need to say on the more positive side? Here the danger is that our characterisation will be a wholly idealistic one, indifferent to the practical limitations which prevent all actual projects from achieving perfection. But perhaps it is a good thing to begin by setting out the goals a researcher might be trying to reach.

One goal will be that of originality. By this we mean the desire to generate or elaborate alternative perspectives, to look at old questions in new ways (and not just produce new data). Another goal will be that of sustained thought and thorough analysis, using procedures that one at least tries to be accountable about. It is also a requirement of good research that it respond to the existing literature on the topic, and engage with the most sophisticated existing formulations – these will not necessarily be the most recent. And finally it is probably a characteristic of good research that it will involve a great deal of care and time if the foregoing requirements are to be met.

In the light of this, we must acknowledge that the requirements of research *qua* research, and not youth work or teaching, will set limits upon the extent to which a project can be planned and run collaboratively, and thus become empowering. There can be quite distinct temporal phases in any research project and questions of empowerment cannot be foregrounded equally at every phase: the 'findings' frequently emerge only after a period of solitary analysis, away from the field and interaction with the informants. The requirements we have outlined are all clearly responsibilities which fall upon the researcher, not upon the *researched*. It would be unrealistic, not to say perverse, to ask the researched to think about the most sophisticated existing formulations of some issue in sociological/linguistic research. Similarly, once a project is committed to engaging with the agenda of the researched (which need not be a research agenda) this may problematise aspects of what the researcher wants to do, or put pressure upon them. We recognise that this is a potential point of tension for empowering research, and that in any particular project there will be compromises. Yet the compromises need not invalidate the research: despite the difficulties, empowering objectives are worth pursuing. In this volume we have tried to explore both the problems and the possibilities.

REFERENCES

Agar, M. (1986) *Speaking of Ethnography*, Beverly Hills, CA: Sage.

Alladina, S. (1986) 'Black people's languages in Britain – a historical and contemporary perspective', *Journal of Multilingual and Multicultural Development*, 7 (5): 349–359.

AAA (American Anthropological Association) (1971) *Statement of Ethics*. (Reprinted in P. Sanday, (ed.) (1976) *Anthropology and the Public Interest*, New York: Academic Press.)

Asad, T. (1986) 'The concept of cultural translation in British social anthropology' in J. Clifford and G. Marcus (eds) *Writing Culture*, Berkeley: University of California Press, 146–164.

Bakhtin, M. (1981) *The Dialogic Imagination*, Austin: University of Texas Press.

Bauman, R. and Sherzer, J. (eds) (1974) *Explorations in the Ethnography of Speaking*, Cambridge: Cambridge University Press.

Bell, A. (1984) 'Language style as audience design', *Language in Society* 13 (2): 145–204.

Berger, P. and Luckmann, T. (1967) *The Social Construction of Reality*, Harmondsworth: Penguin.

Bhavnani, K. (1988) 'Empowerment and social research: some comments', *Text* 8, 1 (2): 41–50.

Bloch, M. (1975) 'Introduction' in M. Bloch (ed.) *Political Language and Oratory in Traditional Society*, London: Academic Press, 1–28.

Bloch, M. (1976) Review of R. Bauman and J. Sherzer (eds) in *Language in Society* 5: 229–234.

Bloor, M. (1978) 'On the analysis of observational data: a discussion of the worth and uses of inductive techniques and respondent validation', *Sociology* 12 (3): 545–552.

Bourdieu, P. (1977) *Outline of a Theory of Practice*, trans. R. Nice, Cambridge: Cambridge University Press.

Bourdieu, P. and Passeron, J. C. (1977) *Reproduction in Education, Society and Culture*, trans. R. Nice, London: Sage.

Briggs, C. (1986) *Learning How to Ask: A Sociolinguistic Appraisal of the Role of the Interview in Social Science Research*, Cambridge: Cambridge University Press.

BSA (British Sociological Association) (1982) *Code of Practice*. (Reprinted in *Network* 43, January 1989.)

Brooks, T. and Roberts, C. (1985) '"No Five Fingers Are All Alike": managing change and difference in the multi-ethnic workplace', in C. Brumfit, R. Ellis and J. Levine (eds) *English as a Second Language in the United Kingdom*, Oxford: Pergamon, 111–130.

Bulmer, M. (1982) *Social Research Ethics*, London: Macmillan.

Bulmer, M. (1984) *Sociological Research Methods – An Introduction*, London: Macmillan.

Bulmer, M. (1980) 'Comment on the ethics of covert research', *British Journal of Sociology*, 31: 59–65.

Cain, M. (1986) 'Realism, feminism, methodology, and law', *International Journal of the Sociology of Law*, 14: 255–267.

Cameron, D. (1989) '"Released into language": teaching linguistics inside and outside academic institutions', in A. Thompson and H. Wilcox (eds) *Teaching Women*, Manchester: Manchester University Press, 5–14.

Cazden, C. (1981) 'Social context of learning to read' in L. B. Resnick and P. A. Weaver (eds) *Theory and Practice of Early Reading*, New York: Lawrence Erlbaum Associates. (Reprinted in N. Mercer (ed.) (1988) *Language and Literacy from an Educational Perspective*, Volume 2, Milton Keynes: Open University Press, 150–162.)

Chalmers, A. (1982) *What is this Thing called Science? An Assessment of the Nature and Status of Science and its Methods*, 2nd edn, Milton Keynes: Open University Press.

Clifford, J. (1988) 'On ethnographic authority' in J. Clifford (ed.) *The Predicament of Culture: Twentieth Century Ethnography, Literature and Art*, Cambridge, Mass.: Harvard University Press, 21–54.

Clifford, J. and Marcus, G. E. (eds) (1986) *Writing Culture: The Poetics and Politics of Ethnography*, Berkeley: University of California Press.

Cole, J. W. and Wolf, E. (1974) (eds) *The Hidden Frontier: Ecology and Ethnicity in an Alpine Valley*, New York: Academic Press.

Connell, R. W. (1987) *Gender and Power – Society, the Person and Sexual Politics*, Oxford: Polity Press.

Coupland, N., Coupland, J., Giles, H. and Henwood, K. (1988) 'Accommodating the elderly: invoking and extending a theory', *Language in Society* 17 (1): 1–42.

Dalphinis, M. (1985) *Caribbean and African Language*, London: Karia.

DES (Department of Education and Science) (1988) *A Survey of the Teaching of English as a Second Language in Six LEAs*, London: HMSO.

Derrida, J. (1976) *Of Grammatology*, Baltimore: Johns Hopkins University Press.

Devonish, H. (1986) *Language and Liberation*, London: Karia.

Dingwall, R. (1980) 'Ethics and ethnography', *Sociological Review* 28 (4): 871–891.

Edwards, V. (1979) *The West Indian Language Issue in British Schools*, London: Routledge & Kegan Paul.

Edwards, V. (1986) *Language in a Black Community*, Clevedon, Avon: Multilingual Matters.

Edwards, V. (1989) 'The speech of British Black women in Dudley, West Midlands', in J. Coates and D. Cameron (eds) *Women in their speech communities*, London: Longman, 33–50.

Erickson, F. (1977) 'Some approaches to inquiry in school-community inquiry', *Anthropology and Education Quarterly* 8 (2): 58–69.

Erickson, F. and Shultz, J. (1981) *The Counsellor as Gatekeeper*, New York: Academic Press.

Fasold, R. (1990) *The Sociolinguistics of Language*, Oxford: Blackwell.

Finch, J. (1984) 'It's great to have someone to talk to – the ethics and politics of interviewing women' in C. Bell and H. Roberts (eds) *Social Researching*, London: Routledge & Kegan Paul, 70–87.

Fishman, J. (1968) *Readings in the Sociology of Language*, The Hague: Mouton.

Fishman, J. (1971–2) *Advances in the Sociology of Language*, The Hague: Mouton.

Fishman, J. (1974) *Advances in Language Planning*, The Hague: Mouton.

Fishman, J. (1978) *Advances in the Study of Societal Multilingualism*, The Hague: Mouton.

Flax, J. (1986) 'Gender as a social problem: in and for feminist theory', *American Studies/Amerika Studien* 31: 193–213.

Foucault, M. (1980) *Power/Knowledge: Selected Interviews and Other Writings 1972–77*, ed. C. Gordon, Brighton: Harvester.

Furnborough, P., Jupp, T., Munns, R., and Roberts, C. (1982) 'Language disadvantage and discrimination: breaking the cycle of majority group perception', *Journal of Multilingual and Multicultural Development* 3 (3): 247–266.

Geertz, C. (1973) *The Interpretation of Cultures*, New York: Basic Books.

Geertz, C. (1988) *Works and Lives*, Oxford: Polity Press.

Giles, H. (1971) 'Our reactions to accent', *New Society*, 14 October, 713–715.

Griffin, C. (1985) *Typical Girls? Young Women from School to the Job Market*, London: Routledge & Kegan Paul.

Gumperz, J. (1982a) *Discourse Strategies*, Cambridge: Cambridge University Press.

Gumperz, J. (ed.) (1982b) *Language and Social Identity*, Cambridge: Cambridge Universtiy Press.

Gumperz, J. and Hymes D. (eds) (1972) *Directions in Sociolinguistics: the Ethnography of Communication*, Oxford: Blackwell; New York: Holt, Rinehart & Winston.

Gumperz, J., Jupp, T., and Roberts, C. (1979) *Crosstalk: A Study of Cross-cultural Communication*, Southall: National Centre for Industrial Language Training.

Hammersley, M. and Atkinson, P. (1983) *Ethnography: Principles in Practice*, London: Tavistock.

Harding, S. (1986) 'From the woman question to the science question', *The science question in feminism*, Ithaca, NY: Cornell University Press, 15–29.

Harding, S. (1987) *Feminism and Methodology – Social Science Issues*, Milton Keynes: Open University Press.

Hart, K. (1990) 'Swimming into the human current', *Times Higher Education Supplement* (18 May).

Harvey, P. (1987a) 'Language and the power of history: the discourse of bilinguals in Ocongate (southern Peru)', Ph.D. dissertation, London School of Economics.

Harvey, P. (1987b) 'Lenguaje y relaciones de poder: consecuencias para una politica linguistica' in *Allpanchis* 29/30: 105–131.

Harvey, P. (1991) 'Drunken speech and the construction of meaning – bilingual competence in the Southern Peruvian Andes', *Language in Society* 20 (1): 1–36.

Harvey, P. (1992) 'Gender, community and confrontation: power relations in drunkenness in Ocongate (southern Peru)' in M. McDonald (ed.) *Gender, Drink and Drugs*, London: Berg.

Heath, S. B. (1983) *Ways with Words*, Cambridge: Cambridge University Press.

Hewitt, R. (1986) *White Talk, Black Talk*, Cambridge: Cambridge University Press.

Hobsbaum, A. (1982) 'Racial bias in research', University of London Institute of Education: unpublished manuscript.

Hollis, M. and Lukes, S. (eds) (1982) *Rationality and Relativism*, Oxford: Blackwell.

Homan, R. (1980) 'The ethics of covert methods', *British Journal of Sociology* 31: 46–59.

Honey, J. (1983) *The Language Trap: Race, Class and 'Standard English' in British Schools*, Kenton, Middlesex: National Centre for Educational Standards.

Hudson, R. A. (1983) 'Linguistic Equality', *CLIE Working Paper* 1.

Hymes, D. (1972a) 'On communicative competence', in J. Pride and J. Holmes (eds) *Sociolinguistics*, Harmondsworth: Penguin, 269–293.

Hymes, D. (1972b) 'Models of the interaction of language and social life', in J. Gumperz and D. Hymes (eds) *Directions in Sociolinguistics: the Ethnography of Communication*, Oxford: Blackwell; New York: Holt, Rinehart and Winston, 35–71.

Hymes, D. (1973) 'Speech and language: on the origins and foundations of inequality among speakers', *Daedalus*, Summer 1973. (Reprinted in D. Hymes 1980: 19–61.)

Hymes, D. (1974) *Foundations in Sociolinguistics: An Ethnographic Approach*, Philadelphia: University of Pennsylvania Press.

Hymes, D. (1980) *Ethnolinguistic Essays*, Washington: Centre for Applied Linguistics.

Jones, S. (1988) *Black Culture, White Youth*, Basingstoke: Macmillan.

Kuper, A. (1977) *Anthropologists and Anthropology: The British School 1922–72*, Harmondsworth: Penguin.

Labov, W. (1969) 'The logic of non-standard English', *Georgetown Monographs on Language and Linguistics* 22, Washington DC: Georgetown University Press. (Also published in W. Labov (1972) *Language in the Inner City*, Philadelphia: University of Pennsylvania Press, 201–240.)

Labov, W. (1972) *Sociolinguistic Patterns*, Oxford: Blackwell.

Labov, W. (1981) 'Field methods used by the project on linguistic change and variation', *Sociolinguistic Working Paper 81*, Austin: South Western Educational Development Laboratory.

Labov, W. (1982) 'Objectivity and commitment in linguistic science: the case of the Black English trial in Ann Arbor', *Language in Society* 11: 165–201.

Lees, S. (1986) *Losing Out: Sexuality and Adolescent Girls*, London: Hutchinson.

Le Page, R. (1980) 'Projection, focussing, diffusion', *York Papers in Linguistics* 9: 9–31.

Le Page, R. and Tabouret-Keller, A. (1985) *Acts of Identity*, Cambridge: Cambridge University Press.

Lévi-Strauss, C. (1978) 'The scope of anthropology', in *Structural Anthropology II*, trans. M. Layton, London: Penguin, 3–32.

Lukes, S. (1974) *Power: a radical view*, Basingstoke: BSA/Macmillan.

Lukes, S. (1986) (ed.) *Power*, Oxford: Blackwell.

Lyons, J. (1968) *Introduction to Theoretical Linguistics*, Cambridge: Cambridge University Press.

McRobbie, A. (1978) 'Working class girls and the culture of femininity' in CCCS Women's Studies Group *Women Take Issue*, London: Hutchinson, 96–108.

Malinowski, B. (1922) *Argonauts of the Western Pacific*, London: Routledge & Kegan Paul.

Malinowski, B. (1926) *Crime and Custom in Savage Society*, London: Routledge & Kegan Paul.

Malinowski, B. (1929) *The Sexual Life of Savages in North Western Melanesia*, London: Routledge & Kegan Paul.

Malinowski, B. (1935) *Coral Gardens and their Magic*, Bloomington: University of Indiana Press.

Malinowski, B. (1967) *A Diary in the Strict Sense of the Term*, New York: Harcourt, Brace & World.

Milgram, S. (1974) *Obedience to Authority*, New York: Harper & Row.

Milroy, J. and Milroy, L. (1985) *Authority in Language*, London: Routledge & Kegan Paul.

REFERENCES

Milroy, L. (1980) *Language and Social Networks*, Oxford: Blackwell.

Milroy, L. (1987) *Observing and Analysing Natural Language*, Oxford: Blackwell.

Morgan, D. (1981) 'Men, masculinity and the process of sociological enquiry' in H. Roberts (ed.) *Doing Feminist Research*, London: Routledge & Kegan Paul, 83–113.

Muehlhausler, P. (1986) *Pidgin and Creole Linguistics*, Oxford: Blackwell.

Muehlhausler, P. (1990) '"Reducing" Pacific languages to writing' in J. Joseph and T. Taylor (eds) *Ideologies of Language*, London: Routledge, 189–205.

Mukherjee, T. (1983) 'ESL: a legacy of failure', *EFL Gazette* 46: 3.

Oakley, A. (1981) 'Interviewing women' in H. Roberts (ed.) *Doing Feminist Research*, London: Routledge & Kegan Paul.

Outhwaite, W. (1987) *New Philosophies of Social Science: Realism, Hermeneutics and Critical Theory*, London: Macmillan.

Rabinow, P. and Sullivan, A. (1979) *Interpretive Social Science*, Berkeley: University of California Press.

Rampton, M. B. (1983) 'Some flaws in educational discussion of the English of Asian schoolchildren in Britain', *Journal of Multilingual and Multicultural Development* 4 (1): 15–28.

Rampton, M. B. (1985) 'A critique of some educational attitudes to the English of British schoolchildren and their implications' in C. Brumfit, R. Ellis and J. Levine (eds) *ESL in the UK*, Oxford: Pergamon, 187–198.

Rampton, M. B. (1987) 'Uses of English in a multilingual British peer group', Ph.D. dissertation, University of London Institute of Education.

Rampton, M. B. (1988) 'A non-educational view of ESL in Britain', *Journal of Multilingual and Multicultural Development* 9 (6): 503–529.

Rampton, M. B. (1989) 'Group affiliation and quantitative sociolinguistics', *York Papers in Linguistics* 13: 279–294.

Rampton, M. B. (1991) 'Interracial Panjabi in a British adolescent peer group', *Language in Society* 20: 391–422.

Rampton, M. B. (1992) 'Language education in policy and peer group', *Language and Education*.

Reason, P. and Rowan, J. (eds) (1981) *Human Inquiry: A Sourcebook of New Paradigm Research*, Chichester: Wiley.

Roberts, H. (ed.) (1981) *Doing Feminist Research*, London: Routledge & Kegan Paul.

Ryan, A. (1970) *The Philosophy of the Social Sciences*, London: Macmillan.

Said, E. (1978) *Orientalism*, New York: Pantheon.

Sapir, E. (1949) *Selected Writings in Language, Culture and Personality*, ed. D. Mandelbaum, Berkeley: University of California Press.

Saville-Troike, M. (1982) *The Ethnography of Communication*, Oxford: Blackwell.

Saville-Troike, M. (1983) 'An anthropological linguistic perspective on uses of ethnography in bilingual language proficiency assessment' in C. Rivera (ed.) *An Ethnographic/Sociolinguistic Approach to Language Proficiency Assessment*, Clevedon: Multilingual Matters, 131–136.

Schegloff, E. (1972) 'Sequencing in conversational openings' in J. Gumperz and D. Hymes (eds) *Directions in Sociolinguistics*, New York: Holt, Rinehart & Winston.

Schiffrin, D. (1987) *Discourse Markers*, Cambridge: Cambridge University Press.

Smith, D. (1986) 'Women's perspective as a radical critique of sociology' in S. Harding (ed.) *Feminism and Methodology – Social Science Issues*, Milton Keynes: Open University Press, 84–96.

Spender, D. (1980) *Man Made Language*, London: Routledge & Kegan Paul.

Stocking, G. (1987) *Victorian Anthropology*, New York: Free Press.

Strathern, M. (1985) 'Dislodging a world view: challenge and counter-challenge in the relationship between feminism and anthropology', *Australian Feminist Studies Journal* 1: 1–25.

Sutcliffe, D. (1982) *British Black English*, Oxford: Blackwell.

Touraine, A. (1981) *The Voice and the Eye – an Analysis of Social Movements*, tr. A. Duff, Cambridge: Cambridge University Press.

Touraine, A. (1983) *Solidarity – the Analysis of a Social Movement, Poland 1980–1981*, Cambridge: Cambridge University Press.

Trigg, R. (1985) *Understanding Social Science: A Philosophical Introduction to the Social Sciences*, Oxford: Blackwell.

Trudgill, P. (1975) *Accent, Dialect and the School*, London: Edward Arnold.

Trudgill, P. (ed.) (1978) *Sociolinguistic Patterns in British English*, London: Edward Arnold.

Trudgill, P. (ed.) (1984) *Applied Sociolinguistics*, London: Academic Press.

Trudgill, P. (1986) *Dialects in Contact*, Oxford: Blackwell.

Trudgill, P. and Giles, H. (1978) 'Sociolinguistics and linguistic value judgments' in F. Coppieters and D. Goyvaerts (eds) *Functional Studies in Language and Literature*. (Reprinted in P. Trudgill (1983) *On Dialect*, Oxford: Blackwell, 201–225.)

Van Dijk, T. (ed.) (1985) *Handbook of Discourse Analysis*, London: Academic Press.

Van Maanen, J. (1988) *Tales of the Field: On Writing Ethnography*, Chicago: University of Chicago Press.

Voloshinov, V. N. (1973) *Marxism and the Philosophy of Language*, New York: Seminar Press.

Wagner, R. (1975) *The Invention of Culture*, Englewood Cliffs, NJ: Prentice Hall.

Walters, K. (1988) 'Dialectology' in F. Newmeyer (ed.) *Linguistics: The Cambridge Survey – IV Language: The Sociocultural Context*, Cambridge: Cambridge University Press, 119–139.

Wardhaugh, R. (1986) *Introduction to Sociolinguistics*, Oxford: Blackwell.

Whyte, H. (1978) *Tropics of Discourse*, Baltimore: Johns Hopkins University Press.

Whyte, W. (1955) *Street Corner Society – the Social Structure of an Italian Slum*, Chicago: Chicago University Press.

Williams, R. (1977) *Marxism and Literature*, Oxford: Oxford University Press.

Willis, P. (1980) *Learning to Labour*, Aldershot: Gower Press.

Woods, J. (1984) 'Groping towards sexism: boys' sex talk', in A. McRobbie and M. Nava (eds) *Gender and Generation*, London: Macmillan, 54–84.

Zentella, A.-C. (1987) 'Language and female identity in the Puerto Rican community', in J. Penfield (ed.) *Women and Language in Transition*, New York: SUNY Press, 167–179.

INDEX